COLLECTED STORIES

COLLECTED STORIES

·A PLAY·

DONALD MARGULIES

THEATRE COMMUNICATIONS GROUP

Library of Congress Catalog-in-Publication Data

Margulies, Donald.
Collected stories / by Donald Margulies.
ISBN 1–55936–152–2. (alk. paper)
1. Biographical fiction—Authorship—Drama.
2. Teacher-student relationships—Drama. I. Title.
PS3563.A653C65   1998
812'.54—dc21   98-14965
CIP

Cover Collage by Donald Margulies
Cover Design and Text Design and Composition by Lisa Govan
First Edition, May 1998
Fourth Printing, May 2010

Collected Stories was commissioned by South Coast Repertory and was developed there as well as at the Sundance Institute Playwrights' Lab in 1995. I am grateful to all the folks at those places, particularly Jerry Patch and Lisa Peterson, both of whom were there at the beginning and helped me find a play amid a motley handful of pages.

Collected Stories received its world premiere at South Coast Repertory (David Emmes, Producing Artistic Director; Martin Benson, Artistic Director) in Costa Mesa, California, on October 29, 1996. It was directed by Lisa Peterson, the set design was by Neil Patel, the costume design was by Candice Cain, the lighting design was by Tom Ruzika and the sound design was by Mitchell Greenhill. The cast was as follows:

RUTH	Kandis Chappell
LISA	Suzanne Cryer

The play was produced in New York City by Manhattan Theatre Club (Lynne Meadow, Artistic Director; Barry Grove, Executive Producer) on April 30, 1997. It was directed by Lisa Peterson, the set design was by Thomas Lynch, the costume design was by Jess Goldstein, the lighting design was by Kenneth Posner and the sound design was by Mark Bennett. The cast was as follows:

RUTH	Maria Tucci
LISA	Debra Messing

Influence is simply a transference of personality, a mode of giving away what is most precious to one's self, and its exercise produces a sense, and, it may be, a reality of loss. Every disciple takes away something from his master.

—OSCAR WILDE
The Portrait of Mr. W. H.

Time is the school in which we learn,
Time is the fire in which we burn.

—DELMORE SCHWARTZ
"Calmly We Walk Through This April's Day"

ACT ONE

· Scene 1 ·

September 1990. Late afternoon. The Greenwich Village apartment of Ruth Steiner, a writer, who looks every bit her fifty-five years. She is reading a short, typed manuscript while dipping mondel bread in tea. A jazz station is on. She makes notes in the margins. The downstairs buzzer sounds. She finishes making her notation. The buzzer sounds again. With no urgency, she gets up, opens the window—with difficulty because it sticks—and calls to the street below.

RUTH: Hello-o-o. Hello? Up here.

LISA *(Three stories below, barely audible)*: Oh, hi! Lisa. Remember?

RUTH: I'm throwing down my key.

LISA: What?

RUTH: The buzzer doesn't work, I'm throwing down my key.

LISA: What? I can't—

RUTH *(Waving a key ring)*: My key, my key! I'm throwing down my key!

LISA: Oh! You want me to let myself in?

RUTH: Yes! *(Mostly to herself)* That's *just* what I want you to do. *(Calls)* I'm throwing it down—back up, I don't want to hit you!

LISA: What?

RUTH: I don't want to *hit* you, back *up*! *(To herself)* Jesus . . . *(She tosses the key ring out the window)* By the tree. The *tree*. No no no. Yes yes!

LISA *(Overlap)*: Got it!

RUTH: Good! 3-F.

LISA: What?

RUTH: Apartment 3-F! F! *(To herself)* As in fucking-can't-believe-this.

LISA: What?

RUTH: F! F! F as in Frank! 3-F! *(She ducks her head back in; to herself)* Is it me or is she deaf? *(She tries to shut the window but it's stuck)* Oh, for God's sake . . . *(Ruth continues to struggle in vain to shut the window)*

(Soon, Lisa Morrison, twenty-six, breathless from her trek upstairs, appears at the front door, which had been ajar all along.)

LISA: Professor?

RUTH *(Her back to Lisa; working on the window)*: Yes yes! Come in!

LISA *(Pushes open the creaky door, sees Ruth)*: Hello! I'm sorry I'm late.

RUTH: That's all right.

LISA: I hadn't checked my mailbox? So I just got your note we were meeting *here* and not in your office like fifteen minutes ago?, and practically *ran* all the way? And then on top of that I got lost . . . ?

RUTH *(Still struggling with the window; preoccupied)*: Mm. Yes. Well.

LISA: You need help with that?

RUTH: Why, yes! As a matter of fact I do. See if you have any better luck with this, will you, dear?

LISA: Sure.

RUTH: The damn thing's warped and I'm freezing.

(Lisa puts her bookbag down on a chair and crosses to the window. Ruth wraps a throw blanket around herself and watches Lisa work on the window.)

LISA: It's stuck.

RUTH: I know it's stuck; it sticks. These goddamn old windows . . .

LISA: Have you got a screwdriver or something?

RUTH: A screwdriver?

LISA: Yeah, *you* know, to like . . .

(Lisa continues to try to maneuver the window while Ruth exits to the kitchen and rummages through drawers.)

RUTH *(Off)*: There's a particular angle, I've found it before . . . You have to . . . If you jiggle it just right . . . My arthritis . . . *(Ruth returns with a metal spatula)* I couldn't find a screwdriver; try this.

LISA: A spatula?

RUTH: Yeah, see if you can . . . *(Lisa wedges the spatula between the window and the frame)* There you go . . . *(Lisa manages to get it closed)* Excellent! Thank you, thank you.

LISA: Hey, no problem; I do windows. *(A small laugh, then)* So. Hi.

RUTH: Hi. *(Picks up Lisa's assignment)*

LISA: It's nice to *be* here. I mean, I was beginning to think I was never gonna find this place.

RUTH: Oh, really? Why? It's not that difficult.

LISA: I know, but you know how you're walking along and all of a sudden West 12th and like West *Some*thing streets intersect?

RUTH: Oh, yes.

LISA: And it's like, "*Wait* a minute?, what is going *on* here?" Like *Alice Through the Looking-Glass* or something.

RUTH: Mm. Yes.

LISA: Anyway, this is such a neat place. It's so nice of you to have me over.

RUTH: Have you over?

LISA: *You* know what I mean.

RUTH *(Continuous)*: I hardly think of this as "having you over."

LISA: I know. I meant . . .

RUTH *(Continuous)*: This isn't exactly a social call.

LISA: I know.

RUTH *(Continuous)*: I *do* this from time to time: meet with my students *here*.

LISA: Uh-huh.

RUTH *(Continuous)*: Mainly because I'm a terrible slug. And if *one* of us has to shlep, it may as well be you; you're younger.

LISA: No, what I meant was, it's so nice to be in a real *home* for a change, where a real person actually *lives*, with real furniture and books and art and stuff? I mean, graduate students? They just don't live in *real* places with *real* histories. My apartment? I mean, it's so makeshift and sad. Milk crate bookcases and ratty old furniture. Completely lacking in *dignity*. And the surfaces are always sticky?, because nobody really cleans up after themselves. *(Ruth is looking at her intently)* What.

RUTH: *You're* Lisa?

LISA: Yes . . . ?

RUTH: Lisa Morrison?

LISA: Uh-huh?

RUTH: *You* wrote "Eating Between Meals"?

LISA: Uh-huh. Why?

RUTH *(Shows her typescript)*: You wrote *this*?

LISA: This is my tutorial, remember we had a tutorial?

RUTH *(Over "... we had a tutorial?")*: Yes yes, I know, but isn't that funny, I thought you were someone else.

LISA: What do you mean?

RUTH: You're not who I thought you were; I confused you with another student.

LISA: Oh.

RUTH: I really should start paying attention to those goddamn seating charts; my memory is shot to hell. I had someone *dark*er in mind. In *all* respects. I decided that Lisa Morrison had to be that *serious* young woman.

LISA: Oh.

RUTH: That mousy Anita Brookner type, the one who never makes eye contact.

LISA *(Thinks, then)*: Janet?

RUTH: That dreary *dark* girl with long bangs that look like she trims them herself by chewing on the ends, who wears those terribly long tartan skirts.

LISA: Janet Spiegel, yeah.

RUTH: *That's* right, *that's* Janet *Spieg*el. Now why did I think she was you? *(Lisa shrugs; a beat)* Hm.

LISA *(Jocularly)*: Are you disappointed?

RUTH: What?

LISA: I mean, that I showed up looking like *me* and not like Janet?

RUTH: No no, it's just that you don't particularly look like your story. Very often, almost without exception, my students tend to *look* like their stories.

LISA: Hm. Isn't that interesting.

RUTH *(Continuous)*: I've prided myself for years for being able to match the student with the story. It's a game I play with myself. I'm so rarely wrong.

LISA *(Self-effacing)*: So you're saying I don't look very serious?

RUTH: What?

LISA: No, that's okay, I'm just curious. You said you thought the person who wrote the story was a *serious*-looking person, that's what you said. So am I *not* a serious-looking person?

RUTH: Young lady . . .

LISA: No, I'm curious. Am I?

(A beat.)

RUTH: No; you're not.

LISA *(Wilts slightly)*: Oh. *(A beat)* But, wait: If you thought the story *I* wrote was written by a serious person . . . Does that mean you thought it was a serious story?

(A beat.)

RUTH: Perhaps. *(A beat)* Can I offer you anything?

LISA: Um, yeah, sure. Thanks.

RUTH: Tea, or . . . ?

LISA: Actually, I would *love* a cup of coffee.

RUTH: Well, actually, I don't *have* coffee.

LISA: Oh.

RUTH: I don't *drink* coffee. I have *tea* . . .

LISA: Oh, okay, I'll have tea.

RUTH: English Breakfast?

LISA: Do you have any herbal?

RUTH: No, I have English Breakfast.

LISA: English Breakfast'll be fine.

RUTH: Good. English Breakfast it is, then. *(She smiles, goes to kitchen)*

LISA *(Calls)*: Thank you. *(She winces to herself at her faux pas; silence; she looks at the bookshelves, picks up an old leather-bound volume)* Oo, what a beautiful edition of *Middlemarch* . . . My copy is falling apart, I've read it so many times . . . *(She briefly looks at it, returns it to the shelf, continues browsing. She finds a story collection by Delmore Schwartz)* Wow, *In Dreams Begin Responsibilities;* I *love In Dreams Begin Responsibilities. (She flips through the book)* I love where he's dreaming he's in the movie theatre watching his parents' courtship on the screen? And just as his father proposes to his mother he shouts out . . . ? *(Finds the passage)* Here it is: *(Reads quickly)* "Don't do it. It's not too late to change your minds, both of you. Nothing good will come of it, only remorse, hatred, scandal and two children whose characters are monstrous." I *love* that. *(Finds an envelope stuck in the book)* Oh my God! Is this letter really from Delmore Schwartz himself?!

RUTH *(Off)*: Put that back, please.

LISA *(Over ". . . please.")*: Oh, I'm sorry . . . *(Flustered, she puts it back)*

RUTH *(Off)*: That's all right, just put it back.

LISA *(Calls)*: Sorry. *(Pause. She sees the book splayed open by Ruth's chair)* Oh, Jane Smiley. Supposed to be really really good. These are novellas, right?

RUTH *(Off)*: Yes.

(Lisa steals a look at Ruth's comments on her typescript. The phone rings. It rings again. She isn't sure what to do.)

LISA: Phone! Hello? Professor? Ms. Steiner? Do you want me to get it?

RUTH *(Off; unperturbed)*: No no.

(The ringing continues. Ruth enters with a cup of tea and snack food on a tray.)

LISA: Oh, thank you! *(The ringing continues)* Is your machine working?

RUTH: My machine?

LISA: 'Cause it's ringing a *lot*. Shouldn't it pick up after like four or five rings?

RUTH: I have no machine.

LISA: Oh. You have no machine? Really? Wow.

RUTH: Why? What do I need a machine for?

LISA: I don't know . . . I mean, I would think, someone as important as you . . . ? God, how do you live without an answering machine?

RUTH: If it's work-related, they'll call my agent. If it's my agent, she'll know to call back later; my friends would know the same.

LISA: What if it's an emergency?

RUTH: I have no children, my parents are dead. What could possibly be so urgent?

(The ringing continues.)

LISA: Look, why don't you just answer it and tell them you'll call them back?

RUTH: I don't want to answer it; why should I answer it? I have company.

LISA: Oh. Who?

RUTH: You.

LISA: Oh. Right.

(The ringing stops.)

RUTH: See that? Couldn't've been *that* important.

(Lisa smiles, samples a piece of mondel bread.)

LISA: Mm. This is good. What is it?

RUTH: Mondel bread.

LISA: Mondel—?

RUTH: Jewish biscotti. *(She demonstrates by dipping the cookie)*

LISA *(Smiles)*: Oh. *(She dips one and spills some tea)* Oo, shit. I'm sorry.

RUTH *(Hands her a napkin)*: That's quite all right.

LISA: You know, I'm really much more together than this—

RUTH: *Are* you.

LISA *(Continuous)*: —but I'm like really really nervous?

RUTH: Are you really? Why is that?

LISA: Why?! Because I can't believe I'm *here*, okay? I can't believe I'm sitting in Ruth Steiner's apartment, on Ruth Steiner's sofa?, sipping tea with Ruth Steiner?, out of Ruth Steiner's china teacups?

RUTH: Oh, come now . . .

LISA: No, I mean, this is where you wrote *The Business of Love*, isn't it?

RUTH: Well, here, and on the Vineyard. A lot of places. On buses, in restaurants, on the Broadway local. But, yes.

LISA *(Refers to a framed print)*: This is the Matisse that hangs over Lydia's bed in "All the Wrong Places."

RUTH *(Impressed)*: Yes.

LISA: I remembered the dancers; she imagines herself dancing with the dancers at the end.

RUTH: That's right.

LISA *(At the window)*: And that's the playground where Joanna's little boy in "The Silent Child" falls and gets a concussion, isn't it?

(A beat.)

RUTH: Well, yes, it is.

(A beat.)

LISA: Eric.

RUTH: Eric?

LISA: The little boy's name: Eric.

RUTH: I'll take your word for it.

LISA: How long have you lived here?

RUTH: You don't want to know.

LISA: Yes I do.

RUTH: A very long time.

LISA: Like ten years?

RUTH: No, more like thirty-one.

LISA: Wow. Thirty-one. So, you wrote every story you practically ever *wrote* here, didn't you?, under this roof, in these little rooms. These are the books you read . . .

RUTH *(Amused by her reverential tone)*: Oh, please . . .

LISA *(Continuous)*: This is the floor you paced. This is the view you saw from your window.

RUTH *(Flattered)*: Oh, knock it off. I think you're going a little overboard, dear, honestly.

LISA *(Over ". . . dear, honestly.")*: Why, you think I'm sucking up to you?

RUTH: Well, it *has* occurred to me, yes . . .

LISA: I don't mean to. What I'm trying to tell you, Ms. Steiner, in my very clumsy stupid way . . . Being here?, studying with you . . . ? It's like a religious experience for me. *(Ruth laughs)* No, really, it *is*. I mean, your voice has been inside my head for so *long*, living in this secret place?, having this secret dialogue with me for like years? I mean, ever since high school when I had to read *The Business of Love* . . . ? I mean, from the opening lines of "Jerry, Darling," that was it for me, I was hooked, you had me. I knew what I wanted to do, I knew what I wanted to be.

RUTH: Oh, dear, I did all that?

LISA: Yes! I read all your stories, all of them, like five or six times? I devoured them. I couldn't get enough, I kept wanting more. I even went to the library?, to look up your uncollected stories?

RUTH: Oh, my, that *is* devotion.

LISA: I sat there one day and read whatever I could find.

RUTH: There's a very good reason why they remain uncollected.

LISA *(Disputing Ruth)*: Oh, no. They all have wonderful things in them. All of them. The three in The *New Yorker?*, the ones in *Ms.* like from the early eighties?, that amazing one in that *Esquire* summer reading issue?, *you* know: the Coney Island lifeguard one? The *Kenyon Review?*

RUTH: Yes yes yes.

LISA: So if I seem like a sycophant or an idiot or something it's only 'cause I'm trying to tell you what a privilege it is to be breathing the same air space as you, that's all. I write much better than I talk so I probably should just shut up.

RUTH: Yes. I mean, yes, you *do* write better than you talk. *(A beat)* Where'd you do your undergraduate work, Lisa?

LISA: In New Jersey?

RUTH: Uh-huh. Where in New Jersey?

LISA: Princeton?

RUTH: Yes, I think I've heard of it. *(Glances at her watch)* Jesus . . . We'd better . . . *(Meaning, deal with the story)*

LISA: Of course.

RUTH: Otherwise I could so easily see myself pissing away my entire afternoon . . .

LISA *(Disarmed, embarrassed)*: Oh, I'm sorry. *(Gets out a notebook and pen)*

RUTH: Just listen first.

LISA: Hm?

RUTH: Why don't you try listening?

LISA: Oh. Okay.

RUTH: Don't immediately start writing down everything I say. Listen. Digest.

LISA: Okay. But what if I forget? I mean, I might forget something you say that's really important.

RUTH *(Over "... really important.")*: If you forget, it probably wasn't worth remembering in the first place. Not everything I say is going to be clever or wise, you know.

LISA: Uh-huh.

RUTH: You may think I'm full of it and that's okay, too. *You're* going to have decide for your*self* what is useful criticism and what is not. I'm not a *doc*tor, you know, I don't dispense prescriptions: If you do such-and-such and such-and-such, your story will be perfect. It doesn't work that way.

LISA: If only it were that easy, huh?

RUTH: I'm not going to tell you *how* to write because I *can't*, I don't pretend to know myself. Writing can't be taught.

LISA: Do you really believe that?

RUTH: As far as I'm concerned, the university is taking your money under false pretenses. *(Lisa laughs) Tal*ent can't be learned; it's innate. People who tell you otherwise are not to be trusted; they're snake oil salesmen, all of them.

LISA: John Gardner said—Did you know him?

RUTH: A little; he wasn't my type.

LISA: Well, he said something like, "Genius is as common as old shoes." Do you think that's true?

RUTH: Oh, that is sheer and utter bullshit. Everybody and his idiot cousin's a goddamn genius: Please. Never pay attention to what writers have to say. Particularly writers who teach. *They* don't have the answers, *none* of us do. The good ones ask the right *quest*ions; that's the key. The ones who aren't so good, well, they have their own agendas, something that usually has to do with ego gratification. All I can do as an artist who teaches, is tell you what I see, feed back to you what I see as a kind of reality test and ask the right questions.

LISA: Do you really resent it?, I mean, having to teach?

RUTH: No! I en*joy* it.

LISA: But don't you hate that it takes you away from your work?

RUTH: I don't mind. I rather like the distraction. For one thing, it gets me out of the house. Which is not a small thing. It gets me talking about what I do—hell, it gets me *talk*ing, period. Otherwise I'd be alone far too much, and remain *si*lent far too much, and I'm alone enough *as* it is. You develop bad habits when you spend too much time alone.

LISA: Really?

RUTH: You're the absolute monarch in your own little kingdom. You have to answer to no one. That's a very dangerous thing for a creative person. Teaching keeps me honest. It keeps my brain active. I'm forced to be critical, to put on my thinking cap. I have to say *some*thing, so I find something to say.

LISA: Is it true you need a new assistant?

RUTH: What?

LISA: I heard you need a new assistant.

RUTH: Yes.

LISA: I heard she graduated and you haven't picked a new one yet.

RUTH: That's correct.

LISA: Can I apply? I mean, are you taking applications or do you already have somebody in mind?

RUTH: No, I don't have anybody in mind.

LISA: Well, then, can I apply?

RUTH: You can do whatever you like. It's not exactly a glamour job. I can be a totally despotic employer.

LISA: I don't care.

RUTH: You don't, huh. Well, look, we've gotten off the track here. We're here to talk about *this*. *(Meaning the manu-*

script) All right? Let's talk about "Eating Between Meals."
(Lisa takes a deep breath) I like your title, by the way.

LISA: Oh, yeah? Thanks.

RUTH: It's a good title. I wish *I'd* thought of it.

LISA: Really? You don't think it's too on the nose? I mean, for a story about bulimia?

RUTH: No, I like it. I think it's got a nice healthy sense of irony.

LISA: Thanks. Yeah, I kind of liked it, too.

RUTH: Do you have a new story in the works?

LISA: Um, yeah, I think I do.

RUTH: Good.

LISA: It's about a divorced dad? Who takes his twelve-year-old daughter to Disneyland with his new girlfriend? And the three of them share a motel room?

RUTH *(Over ". . . share a motel room?")*: Wait wait wait. Don't *tell* me.

LISA: What?

RUTH: Don't tell me about it, write it, I don't want to hear it.

LISA: Oh. Okay.

RUTH *(Continuous)*: Telling takes away the need to write it. It relieves the pressure. And once that tension dissipates, so does the need to relieve it. First write it, then we'll talk about it.

LISA: Okay.

RUTH *(Proceeding)*: Okay, let's see what we've got here . . .

LISA: Um, the story's kind of autobiographical?

RUTH *(Feigning surprise)*: No!

LISA: I guess that was a stupid thing to say, huh? It's obvious, right?

RUTH: It's not that it's obvious, it's inconsequential. I don't care what the basis of a story is as long as it's a good story. But did you *really* stick your finger down your throat like that? I'm joking. Now: Let's look at your opening paragraph.

LISA: Uh-huh.

RUTH: Where your protagonist . . .

LISA: Jessica?

RUTH: Yes, where Jessica goes into the supermarket.

LISA: Uh-huh.

RUTH: Who *is* Jessica?

LISA: Who *is* she?

RUTH: I don't really have a sense yet of who she is. Tell me about her.

LISA: You mean you really want me to . . . ?

RUTH: Yes.

LISA: Oh. Well . . . *(A beat)* Um . . . She was like the baby of her family? Had two older brothers she adored who were like ten and twelve years older?, who babied her to the point of domination and then went away to school and as far as she was concerned abandoned her?, left her all alone to deal with her infantile, incompetent parents just as their marriage was turning into an ugly suburban nightmare? Who was pampered and pretty and all that but felt worthless and undeserving anyway?, and would do anything for attention, even if it meant hurting herself? *(A beat)* Like that. Does that help?

RUTH *(Impressed by what was revealed)*: Yes. *(Reads)* "The automatic door sprang open. I entered into a world of plenty —"

LISA *(Over ". . . of plenty —")*: Wait a second, you're gonna *read* it?

RUTH: Yes.

LISA: Out loud?

RUTH: Yes. Why?

LISA: Oh, it's just, I don't know, I didn't know you were gonna read it *out loud*.

RUTH *(Over "out loud.")*: Lisa, you're going to have to get used to hearing your own words. We're going to begin reading aloud in class next week.

LISA: You mean we're gonna be reading our own stuff?!

RUTH: Yes.

LISA: Oh, God, you're kidding.

RUTH: If *you* can't bear to hear your own words, how can you expect anybody else to?

LISA *(A groan)*: Ugh. I'm a terrible reader. I have a terrible voice.

RUTH: It's not about performance, it's about responsibility, about claiming ownership. That's very very important.

LISA *(Sighs)*: Okay.

RUTH: All right? Are you going to survive this tutorial, or are you going to require oxygen?

LISA: No, I'm okay. *(She closes her eyes)*

RUTH *(Reads)*: "The automatic doors sprang open. I entered into a world of plenty, a cornucopia of temptation, of sustenance and sin, where the music of love was Muzak and anything was possible." *(A beat)* Hm.

LISA: What.

RUTH: Let's think about that phrase for a minute: "anything was possible."

LISA: Yeah . . . ?

RUTH: I don't know, there's something terribly *weak* about that phrase.

LISA: Really? Weak? I'm sorry.

RUTH: "Anything was possible." It feels too general, I think, it's unsatisfying.

LISA: Huh.

RUTH: I like "the music of love was Muzak," I like that. I like "the world of plenty," "cornucopia of temptation," that's all very nice. Just think about that one phrase; give it a little more thought. Good.

LISA: Can I write this down?

RUTH: All right, if you must. Okay. *(Reads)* "I took a red plastic basket from a 'help-yourself' stack and made my way through the crush of harried women pushing shopping carts loaded with unruly toddlers, past precarious towers of brightly packaged foods."

(A beat.)

LISA: What.

RUTH: That sentence. Maybe it's all those bloody adjectives. Look at that: You've got a *shit*load of them: "harried . . . unruly . . . precarious . . ." *Lose* some of them. You don't *need* all that. Less *is* more, for Christ's sake. *(Reads)* "Food was everywhere." Thank God.

LISA: What.

RUTH: A blessed three-word sentence. *(Reads)* "The endless walls of cereal boxes in primary colors made me think of Christmas." Good. Nice. Clean, clear, specific, evocative. *(Increasingly impressed as she reads)* "In the condiment aisle I encountered an overweight little girl, her mouth and pink jogging suit smudged with chocolate, spinning herself around like a sugar-crazed dervish, her mad dance ending only when she dizzily collided with a wall of gherkins. Three glass jars toppled in rapid succession, exploding onto the linoleum like fabulous green water balloons. Shards of glass glistened among the garlic pickles. The girl looked up, saw me, and grinned, delightedly, before taking off down the aisle, leaving her mortified mother and the briny mess behind her." *(Pause. Lisa is smiling, pleased with what she hears. Ruth, impressed, looks at her differently; rereads it to herself; with admiration)* ". . . *Fabulous* green water balloons." Hm. I love that girl. Where did that little girl come from?

LISA: Oh, her? That's me. It's a true story. Only it wasn't pickles, it was ketchup. I thought ketchup might be too, *you* know.

RUTH: Yes. Do you know what you did here? *(Lisa shrugs)* You really don't, do you?

LISA: I don't know, I guess I was struck by this idea of encountering myself as a child? You know? Like this specter in the supermarket? This fat girl with chocolate on her face spinning wildly and making a mess of things and pissing her mother off and not *caring* she was pissing her mother off, but rather en*joy*ing it?

RUTH: Yes. That's right. *(A beat)* Did you have any sense at all as you were writing it: "This is good, this is going well"?

LISA: Oh, I don't know, maybe.

RUTH: Sure you did. You must have. We all experience that. It's part of the thrill. It's when the muse takes over and one is channeling for the muse. *(A beat. Back to the story)* "The ice cream was displayed in a long corridor of frosty glass cases, like precious Etruscan vases in a museum." Now, here I have a question for you. Are you familiar with Etruscan vases?

LISA: Not overly, no. I mean, I've *seen* them?

RUTH: Uh-huh. I would think about that image. Why *Etruscan* vases?

LISA: Why Etruscan?

RUTH: Yes, why not just *ancient* vases or *Greek* vases or whatever? What is it about *Etruscan* vases?

LISA: I don't know, I like the word?

RUTH: Uh-huh. It's a very nice word, isn't it, but why don't you go to the Met and sit with the Etruscan vases for a while and get acquainted with them? See if that's what you really mean to say.

LISA: You mean it?

RUTH: Absolutely. We must never be arbitrary. There is so much goddamn arbitrariness in the world, we mustn't let it seep into our stories. God, not our stories. They're just too damn important. We mustn't devalue our stories with flippancy. That would be the death of us all.

LISA: God, that makes like so much sense? *(Writes in her note-book)*

RUTH: Hm. *(A beat, a breath, a shift)* Um, Lisa?

LISA: Did you not want me to write?

RUTH: No no, that's not it. *(A beat)* Do you mind if I ask you something?

LISA *(Equivocally)*: Uh, okay. Sure.

(Pause.)

RUTH: Why do you talk like that?

LISA: Excuse me?

RUTH: You have a tendency to add question marks to the ends of declarative sentences. Do you know that?

LISA: Oh, God . . .

RUTH: When a simple, declarative sentence will do, you inflect it in such a way . . . When I asked you where you got your bachelor's, you didn't simply say, "Princeton," a statement of fact, you said, "Princeton?" You hear how my voice went up?

LISA: I can't believe I'm still *doing* that; I *used* to talk like that, when I was younger.

RUTH *(Over ". . . when I was younger.")*: I didn't mean to embarrass you, I thought you could shed some light. I'm not saying you do it all the time but you do it often enough for me to notice. And it's very striking because you're obviously an intelligent, gifted young woman but it's really kind of *dopey*, if you ask me.

LISA: It is, it really is; it's awful.

RUTH: You're not alone. Most of my students speak this way. I'm not absolutely certain but I think more young *women* speak this way than young men. And there's something almost *poignant* about it, all these capable young women somehow begging to be heard, begging to be understood. "Can you hear me?" "Are you with me?" "Am I being heard?"

LISA: I know.

RUTH: You've all cultivated this common dialect of American youth. A nonregional, national dialect.

LISA: Uh-huh.

RUTH: Students from the backwoods of Georgia sound the same as students from Chicago, or Great Neck.

LISA: Is it television do you think? *(A beat)* That was a question. I mean, I think it *is* television.

RUTH: Probably. Why not? We blame television for everything *else* that's going to hell in our society, why not this, too?

LISA: It's a vicious circle, I think: Television portrays young people in a certain way, young people watch a lot of television . . . And it's really insidious. Like a media conspiracy to undermine youth or something.

RUTH: But you kids are complicit in this! Role models are *chosen*! You're selling yourselves short!

LISA: By sounding like a bunch of airheads?

RUTH: Yes! Listen to yourselves! Nobody's going to take you *seriously* in the real world! Who's going to take you seriously if you talk like that? No one! Why should they? If I were you, I'd do everything I could to erase it from my memory; expunge it from my speech center. The moment you hear yourself doing it, stop and correct yourself. Pretend I'm your mother telling you to stand up straight: Tell me to drop dead but do it. You'll thank me for it one day, believe me. All right, let's get on with this, we haven't even gotten through the first page.

LISA *(Over ". . . the first page."; blurts, mustering all her courage)*: So do you think I'm any good?

RUTH: What?

LISA: Never mind.

RUTH: Do I think you're any good? *(Lisa nods. A beat)* Well, it's a bit early to say, don't you think?

LISA *(Over "... don't you think?")*: Yeah, but, still, you must have formed *some* opinion by now. I mean, you've been doing this a long time, right?

RUTH: Twenty-odd years.

LISA: Right, so I'll bet your antennae are pretty well tuned. You know it when you see it, right?

RUTH *(Amused)*: This is your first tutorial!

LISA: I know.

RUTH *(Continuous)*: Ask me again six months from now.

LISA: My parents, of course, think this is the most ridiculous thing I've ever done and I've done plenty of things in the realm of the ridiculous, I'd hate to give them the satisfaction. Please, I just need to know if you think I'm wasting my time. Am I? That's all I need to know.

(Pause.)

RUTH: No, I don't think you are. *(Lisa sighs audibly)* I wouldn't *retire* just yet if I were you. You have a lot of work to do. An awful lot. But the *stuff*, I think, is there.

LISA: The stuff? Really? You think I have the stuff?

RUTH: It's very raw, mind you. But yes.

LISA: Oh, God. You're not just saying that?

RUTH: Why would I say something like that if I didn't mean it?

LISA: I don't know, because I'm paying like all this tuition?

RUTH *(Charmed, laughs)*: No, rest assured: I'm a terrible liar. *(Back to the story. Reads)* "My eyes grew wide in the dazzling fluorescence. As I—"

LISA: Is there an actual application form I need to fill out? Or can you just put my name on a list?

RUTH: Again with the job? Young lady, I don't know what you think this job *is*; *I* wouldn't want this job.

LISA: Why not?

RUTH: *Nudg*ing me about this and that, *doc*tor appointments, *con*ferences.

LISA: I can noodge.

RUTH: Listen, it's no great honor, believe me: keeping track of my mail, my schedule; keeping my office from teetering on the brink of chaos, which is where it already is.

LISA: Okay.

RUTH: I assure you, there are a lot better things to do with your time than baby-sit an old fart like me.

LISA: I don't care.

(A beat.)

RUTH: Well, if you really want to apply . . .

LISA: Yes?

RUTH: Apply through the office. Talk to Mrs. Gonzalez.

LISA: Mrs. Gonzalez?

RUTH: She has the applications.

LISA: Okay.

(Ruth shrugs, sips her tea. Pause. She continues reading:)

RUTH: "My eyes grew wide in the dazzling fluorescence. As I reached inside the icy freezer for the Macadamia Brittle, my heart beat quickly in feverish anticipation, as if I were preparing for a tryst with a lover and not for an after school binge." *(A beat)* Nice.

· Scene 2 ·

May 1991. Night. Lisa is puttering in the apartment, sorting through piles of books and papers, making them more orderly. We hear keys jingling at the front door. She excitedly goes to it.

LISA: Oh, hi! Wait! Hold on a sec . . .

(She unlocks the door. Ruth enters carrying overnight bags.)

RUTH: What are you doing here so late?

LISA: I got your mail and watered your plants and stuff and decided to stick around and wait for you. Welcome home! *(Lisa takes her bags)*

RUTH: Thank you.

LISA *(Continuous)*: If you had told me what train you were catching, I would have met you at the station. You wouldn't have had to shlep so much.

RUTH: That's all right. I took a cab.

(She takes off her shoes, walks around in her stocking feet.)

LISA: So! How was Washington? I mean, I *know* how Washington was: You were so fabulous.

RUTH: How do *you* know?

LISA: I saw you on C-SPAN.

RUTH: Oh, God, you're kidding.

LISA: Oh, no, you were so great.

RUTH: Really? How did I look?

LISA: You looked wonderful! You were so poised, and funny. They loved you.

RUTH: Who?

LISA: The committee.

RUTH: How could you tell? It was like talking to a convention of undertakers.

LISA: That was so funny when you said, "*You're* politicians, *I'm* a writer; we all have crosses to bear"? That was so great. You didn't seem nervous at all.

RUTH: I wasn't.

LISA: I would've been a wreck.

RUTH: It's all a show. All of it. I was just playing a part: the feisty older woman who cracks wise and gets away with saying just about anything. If she were alive today, Thelma Ritter would play me in the movies.

LISA: And what you said about "a few inches of immortality on the library shelf"? That was beautiful. God, when you talked about how you nearly gave up writing to work for that plumbing company?! I didn't know that happened.

RUTH: It didn't.

(A beat.)

LISA: What do you mean?

RUTH: It didn't happen.

LISA: But you said . . .

RUTH: Yeah, I know.

LISA: You mean it isn't true?

RUTH: There are *elements* of truth in it—I *did* do office temp work and I *was* offered a full-time job at a plumbing supplies company and I *did* get an NEA grant—but never for a moment did I seriously contemplate giving up writing.

LISA: Well, then, why . . . ?

RUTH: Why did I say that?

LISA: Why did you lie?

RUTH: I didn't lie. I exaggerated.

LISA: Isn't that the same thing?

RUTH: Tell me: Would I have made a compelling case for the National Endowment—before the House of Representatives—if I had simply recounted the facts of my career? Absolutely not. Where's the drama if there's nothing at stake? *(While looking at her mail)* So, using the elements of truth, I spun a tale. I threw a crisis into the mix and allowed myself to be rescued at the eleventh hour by the U.S. Cavalry. I exaggerated. What is art if not an exaggeration of the truth? Made a good story didn't it?

LISA: Oh, yeah, God. *(A beat. Re: the mail)* I sorted everything. Mail that looked important I put here, and everything else . . . Boy, you sure do get a lot of catalogs and junk. More than I do, even. *(Ruth dumps a pile in a wastebasket)* I would've thrown all that out but I wasn't sure if you liked looking at catalogs. I mean, some people do.

RUTH: How long have you been here?

LISA: A few hours. No, more than that. I came over to water the plants and stuff.

RUTH: So you said.

LISA: I stayed and read here a while. I confess. It's a good thing I was here: You got so many calls! So many people were expecting to leave a message on your machine, but then of course I'd have to explain you don't *have* a machine, so then we talked about *that* . . .

RUTH: Who called?

LISA *(Gets messages)*: I couldn't believe it! Norman *Mailer* called, Susan Sontag . . .

RUTH: Oh, yes? How is Susan? I haven't spoken to her in quite a while.

LISA: She seemed fine. I couldn't believe I was *talk*ing to these people! Ed Doctorow. See? *(Shows her that message)* I couldn't believe it, he said, "Tell her *Ed* Doctorow called to send his love and appreciation." "Ed." I was talking to "Ed." It was surreal. All these literary giants on the other end of the telephone! Don't worry, Professor, I tried not to embarrass you. I didn't gush too much—or, at least, I don't *think* I did; I didn't want them to think you'd hired an idiot for an assistant or anything. But they were all really so nice.

RUTH: Are you surprised?

LISA: No. They just seemed so . . . *normal.*

RUTH: I wouldn't go *that* far. *(She begins to stash some letters on her desk but, disoriented by its lack of clutter, stops)* What happened to the pile that was here?

LISA: Oh, I straightened up.

RUTH: Oh, no! Why the hell did you do *that*?!

LISA *(Becoming rattled)*: Remember?, before you left?, I asked if you'd like me to straighten up a little bit?

RUTH *(Over ". . . a little bit?")*: Straighten up, yes. Reorganize my life, no; I did not authorize you to reorganize my life.

LISA *(Over ". . . reorganize my life.")*: I'm sorry . . . I really didn't do anything other than—

RUTH *(Over ". . . other than—")*: I thought "straighten up" meant you were gonna take a *schmatah* and dust! Dusting is something this place could use! How am I supposed to *find* anything now?!

LISA: Just ask me. What are you looking for?

RUTH *(Over "What are you . . .")*: *Ask* you?! I don't want to *ask* you . . .

LISA: I'll tell you exactly where it is. I didn't throw anything out or anything, I just made neater piles.

RUTH: I didn't *want* neater piles, I liked my piles the way I had them.

LISA *(Fighting back tears)*: I'm sorry, I didn't mean to . . .

RUTH *(Continuous)*: There *was* a method to my madness, young lady, which served me well most of my life, thank you very much.

LISA *(Over ". . . thank you very much."; embarrassed, losing it)*: I'm really, really sorry. I was only trying to . . . *(Shuffling papers around)* I'll put everything back the way it was . . .

RUTH *(Takes papers out of her hands)*: Just leave it alone!

(A beat. Lisa crumbles. Afraid that tears might flow, she gets her coat.)

LISA *(Softly)*: Sorry . . .

RUTH: Oh, shit, you're not gonna *cry*, are you . . .

LISA *(Tearfully; heading for the door)*: No . . . Well . . . Good night, Professor. Sorry for any inconvenience . . .

RUTH: Oh, for God's sake . . . *(Calls)* Lisa. Hey. Get over here.

LISA: What.

(Ruth cocks her head; she wants Lisa to come back into the room. Lisa hesitates before she does. Pause.)

RUTH: Thank you for checking my mail and watering my plants.

LISA: You're welcome.

RUTH *(Going to her handbag)*: Let me give you a check . . .

LISA *(Hurt, insulted)*: No! I don't want a check!

RUTH *(Getting out her checkbook)*: No, let me. It was above and beyond the call of duty.

LISA: You don't get it, do you? Put it away. Please. *(Ruth does. A beat. Avoids eye contact)* You know? All I want . . . *(Takes a deep breath)* I want so much to please you. You know? And no matter what I do, it's wrong. I always seem to get your disapproval when it's the opposite I want so badly. All these months, ever since school started, it's been both wonderful and excruciating working for you. I mean, to be so close to you, when I admire you *so* much . . . But every day I see you it's like a test: What *faux pas* will I make? What will I do that'll annoy her *today*?

RUTH *(Compassionately)*: No . . .

LISA: Yes! It's true. There's always something. Some invisible line I've crossed. Or, or something I've bungled out of sheer panic.

RUTH: Panic?

LISA: Yes. You intimidate me so much. When I show you something I've written, or even when I *talk* to you I think, What value could *my* words possibly have to *her*?

RUTH: Oh, dear.

LISA: You're so . . . I mean, I *knew* you were difficult—you *told* me as much. But you really seem to take *pride* in being difficult, though, and that I don't understand. *(Stopping herself)* I've said too much. Look, maybe I'm just not cut out for this, you know? Maybe I'm not. My skin's not thick enough. Oh, well . . . *(She struggles to remove Ruth's key from her key chain and then sets it down)* I'm sorry I touched your things. I thought you would appreciate it; I'm sorry. *(Still not looking at her, she starts to head for the door)* If you're hungry, there's dinner in the fridge.

RUTH: Oh?

LISA: It's nothing. I made a little tuna nicoise, that's all. If you don't like it, that's all right, just throw it out.

RUTH: I'd love a salad.

LISA: Good.

RUTH: Thank you.

LISA *(Nods, then)*: It's in the fridge. So whenever you . . .

RUTH: That was awfully thoughtful of you.

LISA: I figured you'd come home late and everything . . . Well, enjoy it. *(Starts to go)* Good night, Professor. See you in class . . .

RUTH *(Suddenly; stopping her)*: Why don't you join me?

LISA: Oh. No. I couldn't do that . . .

RUTH: Why, do you have other plans?

LISA *(Shakes her head, then)*: Not really.

RUTH: Is there enough for two?

LISA: I suppose.

RUTH: Then why don't you join me?

LISA: Um . . .

RUTH: You wouldn't leave me all alone. Would you? Not on the night of my Washington triumph. Sit down.

(Lisa hesitates, then approaches the table. Ruth picks up the key, hands it back to her and starts for the kitchen.)

LISA: I can do that . . .

RUTH *(Over ". . . do that . . .")*: No, no. Sit. *(Ruth exits. Lisa puts the key back on her chain and sits at the table. Ruth returns with food and plates on a tray. Lisa takes the tray from her. Ruth turns on the radio then joins her)* Oh, this looks perfect! *(They set the table together in silence. Ruth helps herself then passes the bowl to Lisa)* Help yourself. *(Lisa takes the bowl and serves herself. Lights fade as they begin to enjoy their first meal together)*

· SCENE 3 ·

August 1992. About a year later. Sunday brunch. An electric fan is blowing. Ruth is seated; Lisa enters from the kitchen with a tray of iced tea, in the middle of a heated discussion.

LISA: Not only is it appalling that he seduces this . . . *girl* . . .

RUTH: How do you know he seduced her?

LISA: Ruth! Of course he seduced her; he must've seduced her, it wouldn't've taken much; those photographs?! I'm sure she was in awe of him, this famous older man?; he took advantage of her youth and inexperience.

RUTH: Well, that's not very fair to her, is it. She's a thinking, feeling young woman. Isn't it possible they both fell in love?

LISA: Oh, please, Woody's not in love with that girl.

RUTH: How do *you* know?

LISA: How *could* he be? It's all about his narcissistic need for control, that's what it is. *(Ruth laughs)* You know how he finds these women and remakes them in his image? They even start *talk*ing like him. Did you read her interview in *Time*? It's like all her answers were scripted. He put the words into her mouth, I'm sure of it.

RUTH *(Amused)*: *Lis*ten to you.

LISA: Anyway, not only is it appalling that he did it, but that he doesn't seem to think that there's anything *wrong* with it?! That's what's so galling. "No moral dilemmas whatsoever"! Did you see that in here? *(Meaning* Time *magazine)* How could he find "no moral dilemmas whatsoever"?

RUTH: He wasn't looking, so he didn't find any.

LISA: His girlfriend's daughter?!

RUTH: *Ex*-girlfriend's daughter, a*dopt*ed daughter.

LISA: So what? He was still practically a father to her!

RUTH: Not her father, it's not the same.

LISA: Why isn't it? They were together twelve years! Most of this girl's life! If he wasn't her father, her father *fig*ure, then. And what about the twenty-five *other* kids she's got? How do you do that to them? He's fucked up a whole family!

RUTH: Now, now. He says he never looked twice at the girl.

LISA: If you believe that shit.

RUTH: Well, maybe it's true. Maybe she was there all along and he suddenly awakened one day to her irresistible charm.

LISA: What, like *Gigi*? *(Ruth laughs)* Ruth, come on, this is aberrant behavior, don't you think? Hitting on your ex-girlfriend's daughter?

RUTH: When something like this happens, it's hypnotic, it's magnetic, it's irresistible. There is no reason. Reason and morality have nothing to do with it. Particularly when the girl is as naive and impressionable as . . . "My Lai" or whatever her name is. *(Lisa laughs)* The allure of a famous older man is an incredibly powerful thing.

LISA: Well, *that's* provocative, Ruth.

RUTH: Yeah? Well, never mind, you. *(A beat)* Why is gossip so delectable, anyway?

LISA: Gossip's gotten a bum rap. It's a neglected art form. Our new literature. It's got everything: mythology, spectacle, Oedipal drama, morality play . . .

RUTH *(Over ". . . morality play . . .")*: Oh, I don't know, I think it's that we've all got this whopping case of *Schadenfreude*. Gossip is fun. It's fun to watch the mighty stumble and fall. Let's face it. We gawk and gasp and click our tongues but deep down inside we're gloating our asses off.

LISA: I'm not gloating, I'm hurt.

RUTH: Why are you hurt? Why are you so personally affronted?

LISA: Woody was supposed to be the great moralist. The conscience of our age.

RUTH: Bullshit. Who said? A couple of critics? The guy makes some clever movies and already he's the conscience of our age?! Honey, nobody asks to be the conscience of an age. That's a hell of a thing to have to live up to.

LISA: I mean, at the end of *Hannah and Her Sisters*, what did he show us? That domestic happiness was finally possible, even for a loser like him. There was hope for all of us. And now look. It all turns out to have been a sham. I feel so betrayed.

RUTH: How were you betrayed? Lisa! I don't see it. The lines got *blurred*, that's all. You've mixed up the persona with the man. He's entitled to a private life, for God's sake. I don't give a shit what he does in private, I don't want to *know* about it.

LISA: Why are you defending him?

RUTH: I'm not defending him . . .

LISA (*Good-humoredly*): Yes you are. And I'm finding it very irritating, Ruth, I really am.

RUTH (*Over ". . . I really am."*): I want to know why you're so worked up about this. It's more than a movie star misbehaving, obviously. You've forgotten he's a movie star. Movie stars misbehave all the time. Always have. That's what they do. That's why we invented them: So they could act out for all of us. It's not the misbehavior. It's what it represents.

LISA: Oh, thank you, Dr. Freud. So what are you saying? I'm still pissed at my father for leaving my mother?

RUTH: Uh, well . . . Now that you mention it, darling . . .
(*Bingo*)

LISA: All right, so? *(A beat)* I went over all this with my shrink yesterday. A whole session on Woody, Mia and Daddy Dearest.

RUTH: Can you imagine the therapeutic impact Woody's little indiscretion is going to have? *Thou*sands of people, lying on couches, all over Manhattan, moaning to their analysts about it?

LISA: I couldn't be*lieve* the shit that poured out. Feelings of rage, betrayal, abandonment. Like I was twelve years old all over again. My father isn't talking to me, by the way.

RUTH: Oh, really, why?

LISA: I don't know. *(A beat)* I gave him the Disneyland story to read.

RUTH: Oh, dear.

LISA: Yeah, and he hated it.

RUTH: Well, that's no surprise.

LISA: He was furious. "Katherine was so upset, she cried. How could you do that to her?" I didn't give the story to *Kath*erine to read, I gave it to *him*. "Why would you want to hurt us like this? She's only gone out of her way to be nice to you," blah blah blah. Oh, God, it was horrible. I never should've written it.

RUTH: Well, that just wasn't an option; you *had* to write it.

LISA: Didn't I?

RUTH: Absolutely. The question is: Why'd you give it to him to *read*? Hm? It's not a very flattering portrait.

LISA: I know.

RUTH *(Pokes at her affectionately)*: So why'd you give it to him?

LISA: I don't know, I wanted him to read it.

RUTH: Why?

LISA: So he'd have *some* idea of what I'm doing. He has no idea. He hasn't read my stuff since high school.

RUTH: Well, the Disneyland story was a pretty tough introduction to your work, don't you think?

LISA *(Over "...don't you think?")*: Yeah yeah, I suppose so. But I didn't want to be *secret*ive about it, that didn't feel right, either. I thought I was doing the right thing.

RUTH: What did you hope to accomplish? *(Lisa shrugs)* To gain his respect?

LISA *(Mostly to herself)*: I don't know...

RUTH: His approval? To show him what a good little writer you are?

LISA: I guess. Yeah; that's ex*act*ly what I wanted: I wanted his approval. Pretty infantile, huh?

RUTH: Well, then why'd you give him this particular story? I mean, you could've given him one of the more *benign* stories to read if you were interested in having him read something, couldn't you?

LISA: Yes...

RUTH *(Continuous)*: But you chose to go right for the jugular and I think that's very interesting.

LISA: If I'm gonna write what I know, it's inevitably gonna hurt some peoples' feelings, right?, somebody's feelings are gonna get hurt.

RUTH: True, that's a risk you're just gonna have to take. You can't censor your creative impulses because of the danger of hurting someone's feelings.

LISA: Even if it's my father's?

RUTH: Even if it is. If you have a story to tell, tell it. Zero in on it and don't flinch, just do it. You know the photographer Robert Capa? He took that famous picture of the falling soldier during the Spanish Civil War?

LISA: Oh, yeah.

(They both briefly mime falling backward.)

RUTH: Right. He said about his work, "If it isn't good enough, I didn't get close enough." And the same could be said for fiction. You've got to get in there and shoot. I guess what *I* want to know is: *(A beat)* Why'd you show him a story he never had to see?

LISA: Well, actually, he *would* see it; this was sort of a pre-emptive strike.

RUTH: Oh?

(A beat.)

LISA: It's being published.

RUTH: It is? *(Lisa nods)* How did *that* happen? I mean, I thought we'd already heard from everyone we'd sent it out to.

LISA: We did. *(A beat)* I also sent it to *Grand Street*.

RUTH: *Grand Street*. Really. But I thought we'd decided *not* to send it to *Grand Street*.

LISA: We did.

RUTH: I thought we'd decided that wasn't exactly the right journal for it. And I didn't know anybody there.

LISA: Right. But I decided to send it in anyway, just for the hell of it, and see what happened.

RUTH: Oh. *(A beat)* But what about a letter? You didn't ask me to write them a letter, did you?, because I don't remember . . .

LISA *(Over ". . . because I don't remember . . .")*: No, I just sent it. With a cover letter of my own, *you* know, the basic.

RUTH: Well! And they're publishing it?

LISA: Uh-huh. That's what they said.

RUTH: Well, how do you like *that*?!

LISA: Yeah.

RUTH: I never would have guessed they'd go for it; it didn't seem like their cup of tea at all.

LISA: I know; that's what we thought.

RUTH: Well, congratulations!

LISA: Thanks. It'll be in the winter issue. Not the fall, but the winter. Out in December.

RUTH: Well, isn't that nice! You'll be a published writer.

LISA: I know.

RUTH: Congratulations.

LISA: Thank you.

RUTH: Your first published story. Isn't that wonderful!

LISA *(Over "Isn't that . . .")*: Yeah, I can't believe it.

RUTH: Well, we'll have to celebrate.

LISA: Yes. Let's.

(A beat.)

RUTH: What did they do? Call you?, write you?

LISA: They wrote me.

RUTH: Uh-huh. When?

LISA *(Shrugs it off)*: The other day.

RUTH *(Nods; a beat)*: I've spoken to you every single day this week and I didn't hear a word about a letter from *Grand Street.*

LISA: I just found out.

RUTH: The other day, you said.

LISA: I don't remember *when* exactly; what difference does it make?

RUTH: Well, it *is* sort of curious. I mean, why didn't you call me immediately?

LISA: What?

RUTH: Why wasn't I the first person you called?

LISA: Oh, Ruth . . . Maybe you *were.* You'd never know: If you'd bother to get a machine . . .

RUTH: Oh, so you're saying you *did* call me?, or you *might* have called me?

LISA: Ruth, I don't understand this.

RUTH: I just think it's very curious, dear: The person most invested in your progress and you wait till *now* to tell me? In a most roundabout way, I might add.

LISA: Ruth, you're reading way too much significance into all this.

RUTH: Am I?

LISA: I'm telling you *now*; I told you *today*. I wanted to tell you face-to-face.

RUTH: I thought you said you tried calling me.

LISA: You're impossible, you know that?

RUTH: *Did* you? *Did* you try calling me? Or was that a convenient lie?

LISA: Why would I lie?

RUTH *(Picks up the* Times Book Review *to read)*: Well, I don't think you're being totally upfront with me.

LISA *(Confused; takes away the paper to continue the discussion)*: Ruth . . . ?

RUTH: What's the matter?, you didn't think I could take it?

LISA: What?!

RUTH: You were cushioning the blow?

LISA: What blow?

RUTH: You thought I'd be threatened by your success?

LISA: No! *(A beat)* I didn't tell you . . . I felt a little funny, I guess, because I submitted it on my own.

RUTH: But you'd hoped, of course, they'd accept it.

(They are looking at one another. Ruth is enraged; Lisa is incredulous.)

LISA: What?!

RUTH: Admit it!

(Ruth snatches back the Book Review *and resumes reading it. Silence.)*

LISA: It's just a little journal; nobody really reads it anyway.

(Lisa waits for Ruth to respond, but she doesn't say any-thing. The phone rings four times; neither answers it. An extended silent sequence follows in which Ruth reads, sips iced tea; Lisa stretches out on the sofa with her back to Ruth, flips through the Sunday Magazine, *works on the puzzle, nibbles on a bagel, etc. Ruth, feeling a bit remorseful, glances at Lisa but continues reading. Lisa sits up. After a pause:)*

Ruth? *(A beat)* Tell me about Delmore Schwartz?

(A beat.)

RUTH: What?

LISA: I want to hear about you and Delmore Schwartz.

RUTH: What are you talking about?

LISA: Tell me.

RUTH: I don't know what you're talking about.

LISA: He was your famous older man, wasn't he.

RUTH: Oh, for God's sake . . .

LISA: Wasn't he, Ruth.

RUTH: I never said any such thing.

LISA: I know, but he was, wasn't he.

RUTH: How did you get *that?*

LISA: It didn't click, till just now. When we were talking about Woody . . .

RUTH: Oh, that's ridiculous.

LISA: I'm right, aren't I? *(Ruth scoffs)* Ah-ha. I am. I can tell. *(Teasing)* Come on, Ruth . . .

RUTH: What do you *want* from me?

LISA: I want you to tell me.

RUTH: There's nothing to tell.

LISA: Ruth . . .

RUTH: It's really none of your business.

LISA *(Laying off)*: All right. *(A beat)* Look, if you don't want to tell me, that's okay, I understand. I was only trying to get you to talk to me. But if you don't want to tell me . . . I understand. No, really.

(Pause. Lisa returns to the puzzle. After a moment, Ruth, distracted, takes off her glasses.)

RUTH: Ach, it was a *mil*lion and one years ago. *(A beat. Lisa puts down the* Magazine*)* Another lifetime. *(Pause)* I . . . I was quite young.

LISA: How young?

RUTH *(Sighs, then)*: Twenty-two. *(Pause)* But a young twenty-two. *(A beat)* An innocent in many ways. A virgin. I was a *good* girl, a nice Jewish girl, a *passion*ate girl, one of those passionate, virginal girls who'd read Dickinson and Hopkins and sob her eyes out. Poetry was my love, my romance, my religion. What a time.

(Pause.)

LISA: When was this?

RUTH: '57, '58. The city was teeming with beatnik poets and old lefties. Smoky bars and late-night sessions. Every once in a while you'd glimpse a Ginsberg, or a Berryman, on the street, in a bookstore—the Eighth Street, the Gotham or the Strand—and the rush of possibility would intoxicate you and keep you plodding along for days and weeks—until your *next* close encounter. *(A beat)* I'd just come to the city from Detroit, to be a poet, of course, and took an apartment, a tiny walk-up, on

Grove Street, above an Italian restaurant. The place smelled of garlic. Always. It was wonderful. My pillow smelled of garlic, my clothes. I had a roommate named Elaine, who was also from Detroit, the daughter of a friend of a family friend and an aspiring actress who would soon marry a rich man and give up her dream forever and die of breast cancer at thirty-nine, and the only soul I knew in all of New York City. *(A beat)* One sleeting night, Elaine shlepped me into a bar on Hudson Street—The White Horse Tavern—and there, sitting in a booth, his wide handsome moon face shining, his big voice booming for all to hear whether they liked it or not . . . There, performing for the two adoring pretty coeds who sat at his table . . . There, was the great poet Delmore Schwartz, mad prophet, squandered genius, "son of Europe, America and Israel."

LISA: Oh, Ruth, this is incredible.

RUTH: We sat across the aisle, Elaine and I, and he included us in his rant, I don't know, about DiMaggio one minute, Kierkegaard the next. After midnight, the first team of cheerleaders grew tired and left, and Elaine and I moved our drinks into his booth. Seeing his shining face across the table now, his eyes darting about, gleaming with brilliance . . . There was so much going *on* in there. And he was already way past his prime at this point. He was gray and bloated and going to seed. His overcoat reeked of stale smoke and his teeth were baked yellow from tobacco. That enormous head with those widely spaced eyes. There was still something magnificent about him. He had been quite beautiful, once.

LISA: I know, I've seen pictures.

RUTH: So, yes, the power was undeniable. *(A beat)* He was only forty-four but there was something ancient about him, something terribly mortal and immortal at the same time, if that makes any sense. He seemed to possess so much wisdom and yet, even then, even that first sleeting night, he seemed doomed. *(A beat)*

What sheltered Jewish girl from Detroit, what self-styled poet, what virgin, would *not* have succumbed? *(Lisa shakes her head)*

And I was pretty then, too.

LISA: I'm sure; I know.

RUTH: You've seen pictures.

LISA: Yes!

RUTH: Well, pretty enough. Shapely, anyhow. I looked damn good in those tight, coed, Lana Turner sweaters. I was good company for a man like Delmore. Being my father's daughter had provided me with years of practice. I was a good listener but I also had a real mouth on me, which he'd point out frequently, with pleasure. I would tease him, provoke him, take outrageous positions just to get a rise out of him, which I always did. *(Pause)* I stuck by him for over a year but he was descending rapidly by then. He was quite mad, you know. Oh, he had his moments—lucid, marvelous moments—but, when they came, the rampages were fiercer and fiercer. He could be cruel, inconstant. His *aura* sustained me. *(A beat)* I'd go to his awful rented rooms while he was out—*you* know: sordid furnished rooms with a sink and a hot plate—and I'd wash the dishes that piled up for days and clean up his mess and mend his clothes and he'd come in . . . and never say a word of thanks. One day I let myself in and found *another* bright-eyed girl lovingly washing his socks in the sink. "Oh," she said, surprised to see me. I turned around and left and never came back. *(A beat)* You probably know the rest of the tale: how he was staying in one of those hotels when he died in '66; how his body lay unclaimed in the morgue for days. *(Pause)*

The years pass and the years pass
& still I see only as in a glass
darkly and vaguely —-
waiting, in "grinding misery"
for the fountain of poetry
to flow and overflow once again.

(Pause.)

LISA *(A sigh)*: Wow.

RUTH: Poor schmuck. *(Pause; suddenly saddened)* I don't talk about this; why'd you make me talk about this?

LISA *(Over "... talk about this?"; gently)*: I'm sorry.

RUTH: It's too painful conjuring up that girl, that affair. I sewed that man's trousers. I held him when he woke up in a cold sweat. I took lots of shit from him in the name of poetry. I'm not particularly proud of all that happened and yet . . . it *was* my shining moment.

LISA: No; it wasn't.

RUTH *(Looking right at her)*: It *was*. It *was*.

(Pause.)

LISA: And you've never written about it. *(Ruth shakes her head)* Really. *(Ruth nods)* How come?

RUTH: Some things you don't touch. *(Long pause)* Listen, I don't mean to be a big, old baby. *(Ruth, in a conciliatory gesture, goes to Lisa)*

LISA *(Approaching her)*: Oh, Ruth . . .

RUTH: You know I'm happy for you, don't you?

LISA: Of course I know that.

RUTH: I'm very very proud.

LISA: I know. I know.

(Ruth envelops Lisa with her arms and holds her very tightly. She is distracted; her smile fades. Silence.)

ACT TWO

· SCENE I ·

December 1994. Nearly two and a half years later. Early morning. Ruth is seated, reading the book page of the daily New York Times; *Lisa, still wearing her coat, restlessly monitors Ruth's reaction. Long silence.*

RUTH *(Barely audible)*: Mm.
LISA: What.
RUTH: I was clearing my throat.

> *(Silence. Ruth puts down the paper and looks at Lisa. A beat.)*

LISA: Well . . . ?

> *(A beat.)*

RUTH: It's good.
LISA *(With trepidation)*: Yeah?
RUTH: It's very good.
LISA: Oh, God.
RUTH: Do you want me to read it to you or not?
LISA *(Over "... or not?")*: No no no. Just the highlights.

RUTH: The highlights, huh? *(Looks over the review)* Well, the closing paragraph is to die for.

LISA: It is?

RUTH *(Offering the paper)*: You're sure you don't want to—?

LISA: No no no. I want *you* to.

RUTH *(Reads from the review)*: "Despite the occasional misstep—"

LISA: Oh, shit, wait, there are missteps?

RUTH: Minor, minor, not to worry. *(Continues)* "Despite the occasional misstep, Ms. Morrison's is a distinct, albeit youthful, voice that must be reckoned with."

LISA: Oh, God . . .

RUTH *(Continuous)*: "In the dozen compact, well-observed stories that comprise *Eating Between Meals*, she proves herself a keen and clever chronicler of the new lost generation." *(A beat)* Well!

(Silence.)

LISA: What was that?, ". . . keen and clever . . ."?

RUTH: "Keen and clever chronicler." *(Lisa takes the paper, looks it over)* Our Michiko seems to have been bit by the alliteration bug.

LISA *(A beat; reads)*: "As in Tolstoy"—whoa!—"the unhappy families in Ms. Morrison's universe are uniquely compelling."

RUTH: All right all right, maybe you *shouldn't* read it; you'll start believing that shit.

LISA *(Pause; still looking over the review)*: Okay, so she doesn't like "Family Reunion."

RUTH: Mm. Neither did I.

LISA: She says I try too hard.

RUTH: Yes.

LISA: It's "stylistically self-conscious."

RUTH: I wasn't gonna say I told you so, but . . .

LISA *(Still on the review)*: Oh, good, she likes "Disneyland." *(Rushes through)* "A harrowing story in which a pubescent girl is forced to confront her father's sexuality." That's good.

(Pause. Lisa reads silently.)

RUTH: You know what the problem with that story was?

LISA *(Still reading)*: Hm?

RUTH: That *story*.

LISA: What story?

RUTH: "Family Reunion." It was too fancy. All those interior monologues for all the members of the family: You didn't need all that. Remember I told you?

LISA: I thought you weren't gonna say I told you so.

RUTH: It *is* stylistically self-conscious; she's right.

LISA *(Tuning her out, still reading to herself)*: Uh-huh.

(A beat.)

RUTH: You know how it came off? It came off as a young writer showing off some pyrotechnics just to prove how versatile she is.

LISA *(Somewhat annoyed)*: Okay! *(Silence while Lisa finishes reading. She puts down the paper. She seems depressed. Softly)*: Wow.

RUTH: How do you feel?

LISA: I don't know yet.

RUTH: That's a splendid review, you know; it doesn't *get* much better than that.

LISA: I know.

RUTH: Your life will never be the same, you know, from this morning on.

LISA: Thank you very much.

RUTH: Now when they print their lists of promising young writers, *you'll* be on them.

LISA: Oh, God.

RUTH: You're on the map. Yesterday you were undiscovered country, today you're on the map. *(She takes Lisa's hand. Genuinely)*: Good for you, sweetie.

LISA: Why do I feel so awful?

RUTH: That's understandable. There's nothing worse than getting what you wanted. *(Getting up)* Now: What do I have that we can toast with? . . .

LISA: It's not even nine in the morning!

RUTH: *(Exiting to kitchen)*: So what? We have to celebrate. *(Off)* After *The Business of Love* came out, you know, I was a total mess.

LISA *(Calls)*: You were?

RUTH *(Off)*: Oh, God, yes. I sank into a terrible depression.

LISA: Really?

RUTH *(Comes back in)*: I thought I had a bottle of champagne but it's one of those sparkling ciders somebody brought to Thanksgiving years ago that nobody ever drinks. Do you mind?

(Lisa shakes her head; Ruth returns to the kitchen.)

LISA *(Calls)*: You really got depressed?

RUTH *(Off)*: Oh, yeah. It took me months, maybe *years* to get over it—that is, if I ever truly did. It was a terrible shock: recognition. I was so inured to living in obscurity, writing my little stories and shipping them off to these tiny esoteric journals. I thought I was looking at the rest of my life. *(Returns with glasses and opens the bottle)*

I'd given up hope. *No* hope was the code by which I lived. It was strangely comforting; it left little room for disappointment. I was a bit older than you, you know, a rather late bloomer compared to you. The *Times* played me up quite a bit. I was hailed as "a brave new voice," "an urban balladeer." I had my "finger on the pulse of the city," they said, or some such nonsense.

LISA: Uh-huh.

RUTH: They put me on the cover of the *Book Review* with a picture of me wearing these terrible—I can't believe I ever wore them—harlequin-like glasses. There I was, the new lady writer of the moment, smiling painfully, at my desk, not knowing *what* to do with my hands. *(A beat)*

(In conclusion, as she pours) You've got to view this purely as an economic development. Maybe some grants will start to come your way, some neat opportunities. And that's very nice. But the fact remains you still have to do the work and you still have to put up with assholes. Only *now* doing the work will be harder, and the assholes you'll have to put up with'll be of a slightly higher-echelon of assholes. And, that, as far as I can tell, is the definition of success.

(She raises her glass. A beat) To perseverance, hard work—and Michiko Kakutani.

LISA: Amen. *(They drink. Pause)* I couldn't've done it without you, Ruth.

RUTH: I know, I know.

LISA: I mean it.

RUTH: I know, dear, so do I.

(Lisa smiles. Pause.)

LISA: So, what do I do now?

RUTH: You'll do what you need to do.

LISA: I don't know what that is.

RUTH: It'll come. You'll figure it out.

LISA: How long should I give it?

RUTH: How ever long it takes.

LISA: What if it never comes?

RUTH: Lisa . . .

LISA: What if this is it?

RUTH: Come on . . .

LISA: No, seriously. What if I'm a one-book wonder?

RUTH: Oh, please . . . You're *not* . . .

LISA: How do you *know*? What if I'm not really a writer after all?

RUTH *(Over ". . . after all?")*: Lisa! Jesus! Stop doing this to yourself!

LISA: Everything I've tried to write, all these weeks, waiting for the book to come out . . . I don't know, I've got to come up with something *big*ger than myself, you know? Out*side* of myself. I've got to get out of the suburbs. I need to get away from people my own age. It's hell being "the voice of a generation."

RUTH: That title is, what?, five minutes old?

LISA: I've blown the lid off bulimia in the suburbs. Whoopee. Big news, right? What do I do for an encore? It all seems so small now, so puny.

RUTH: What does?

LISA: My whole world. *You* know: disaffected youth, disaffected parents. Sex and drugs in the family room. Uh . . . Mother drinks, father cheats. What else? Oh, yes: Sorority sister makes a pass at a party—too much to drink and a kiss in the pool. You name it, I've told it all. Crammed everything I know into a mere hundred-and-eighty-six pages. And that's with title pages and like a large-print-edition typeface that I find really embarrassing. *(A beat)*

It's pathetic. I looted my diaries for tasty morsels. My frenzied, angst-ridden, adolescent jottings: I stole whole chunks.

RUTH: We're all rummagers. All writers are. Rummagers at a tag sale. Picking through the neighbors' discards for material, whatever we can get our hands on. Shamelessly. Why stop at our own journals?

LISA: Well, the truth is, I'm not so angry anymore—I mean I'm in "treatment," okay?, and moved to *Chel*sea, so *now* what do I do? I've *done* my parents. I've *done* my family. I'm not *angry* with them anymore. *Fuck* them. I write all *day*, allegedly. I don't *see* anybody, I don't *go* anywhere because I'm allegedly writing all the time. My boyfriend's a *lawyer*; need I say more? My *friends* are all boring because they're all in exactly the same place I am. My life?, I have no life. Every little quasi idea that pops into my brain seems so banal, so *television*. *(A beat)*

So, I spend my days writing alleged stories about creatively paralyzed women in their twenties who live in cramped but cozy Chelsea apartments. *(A beat)*

You were lucky.

RUTH: Why was I lucky?

LISA: You had all that rich, wonderful, *Jewish* stuff to draw on.

RUTH: Why was that luck? That was what I knew; I started out writing what I knew, just like you and everybody else who writes.

LISA: Yeah, but that culture!, that history! The first-generation American experience and all that. Nothing in my experience could possibly approach that. What do *I* have? *WASP* culture. Which is no culture at all.

RUTH: Oh, really? Tell that to Cheever and Updike.

LISA: Oh, God, I've got to write a novel, don't you think? Isn't that what they want?

RUTH: Who?

LISA: Isn't that what they expect? The literary establishment. I mean, in order for me to be taken seriously?

RUTH: Why? *I* never did.

LISA: Yeah, I know, but don't you think that hurt you?

RUTH *(Bristles slightly; a beat)*: Hurt me?

LISA *(Backpedaling)*: I mean, not *hurt* you, but don't you think it affected you?, affected your reputation?

RUTH: No.

LISA: Oh. Okay.

(Pause.)

RUTH: Why? Do *you* think it did?

LISA: No, I just thought that maybe *you* felt that way.

RUTH: No. I don't. Why? Have I ever *said* as much?

LISA: No, it's just, as I see it, and maybe I've got it all wrong, but as *I* understood the game, the well-received first *collection* is like a rite of passage; the well-received first *novel* is coming-of-age. It's arrival, acceptance. Proof that you weren't a fluke.

RUTH: I don't know who came up with those rules. But *I* certainly never played by them. As far as I'm concerned, a writer is a writer, no matter *what* form that writing takes.

LISA: I don't know, I think this is the playing-with-the-big-boys thing of mine. *You* know, that I can't possibly play with the big boys? Probably has something to do with my father always telling me how I couldn't *do* things. This subtle form of sexism. Not so subtle, really, sub*versive*. *(A beat)*

I mean, I feel as if I've *said* it all already, everything I could possibly have to say, I've already said it, in twelve, what did she call them?, "compact, well-observed stories."

RUTH: Uh-oh, memorizing your reviews. I knew it.

(Pause.)

LISA: What if the Sunday *Book Review* hates it?

RUTH: Honey, relax, they might not even review it. Or if they do, it might be one of those perfunctory little blurby things that nobody pays attention to anyway.

(Pause.)

LISA: The advance word must be pretty good. *Publishers Weekly* and *Kirkus? They* liked it.

RUTH: Uh-huh.

(Pause.)

LISA: And *Mirabella*'s doing a piece on me, did I tell you?

RUTH: No. See?

LISA: They want to take my picture. Should I let them?

RUTH: Why not?

LISA: I don't know, it doesn't seem right. I should be writing, I shouldn't be doing photo shoots.

RUTH: What the hell? It's only a picture. It might be a damned good picture. Enjoy yourself. As long as you don't wear harlequin glasses.

(Pause.)

LISA: I wonder if they'll let me keep the clothes.

RUTH: Lisa!

LISA: You know how you hear how men can't handle success? Men get famous and it's all about sex? I get *my* first little taste of fame and all I can think about is shopping.

(Pause.)

RUTH: Tell me—I've got to ask you something.

LISA: What.

RUTH: Maybe this isn't the right time . . . It's your day . . .

LISA: No, tell me, what.

(A beat.)

RUTH: Do you realize it's been over a week since I gave you my new story and you haven't said a *word?*

LISA *(Over ". . . and you haven't . . .")*: Oh, shit, I know I know, I'm sorry I'm sorry . . .

RUTH *(Over ". . . I'm sorry . . .")*: I know this seems really selfish and inappropriate of me . . .

LISA *(Over ". . . and inappropriate of me . . .")*: No, no, not at all.

RUTH: I *gave* it to you because I was anxious to hear what you thought.

LISA: I know, and I was incredibly honored that you did.

RUTH: Ah, well, but you've probably been too busy and distracted and haven't had the time to . . .

LISA: Well, actually, I *did* read it.

RUTH: You did? *(Lisa nods)* Oh.

LISA: I read it the night you gave it to me. I liked it very much.

RUTH: Then why the hell didn't you *tell* me, you little shit?! Instead of making me twist slowly?!

LISA: I don't know, I didn't *mean* to. I didn't know what to say.

RUTH: How about "I liked it"? That would've been great for starters.

LISA: I mean, I wasn't sure of the protocol.

RUTH: Protocol?! With *me*?!

LISA: I felt shy. You'd never given me a new story of yours to read and asked me what I thought before.

RUTH: Well, things are different now. The morning paper confirms it, doesn't it? We're colleagues now. So, tell me: What did you think?

LISA: I told you.

RUTH: All right, so you liked it. What did you like about it?

LISA: Ruth . . .

RUTH: Come on, kiddo, "voice of a generation," speak.

LISA: I liked the characters. The mother and daughter.

RUTH: Did you find them believable?

LISA: Totally.

RUTH: Why?

LISA: It's what you do, Ruth, like nobody else: the way you capture the essence of relationships. I mean, the structure is so brilliant: these two women squabbling in the kitchen over the years, while baking birthday cakes? You're amazing.

RUTH: Cut the flattery. I wasn't fishing, I want to know what you thought.

LISA: You really do.

RUTH: Yes.

LISA: Okay. *(A beat)* I had problems with it.

RUTH: Ah. Well. Now we're getting somewhere. What kind of problems?

LISA: Well. You do such a beautiful job of creating these quirky, utterly recognizable women—I saw a lot of myself in Emily, actually.

RUTH: Huh!

LISA: And then, I've got to say, I felt really manipulated and disappointed by the ending.

RUTH: Oh? Disappointed? How?

LISA: I mean, sentimentality is not your thing; it never has been. It's such a wonderful story but giving the mother a terminal illness . . . You didn't have to do *that*.

RUTH: Really.

LISA: You begin to fall in love with Martha, even when she's being hypercritical of everything Emily tries to do; I mean, she even has something to say about the way

Emily pours the *vanilla*, for God's sake. But she's funny and honest, and Emily seems to know how to hold her own with her, and they're fun to eavesdrop on as Emily grows up and Martha grows old. So when you don't *take* them anywhere, and don't *resolve* the relationship between them . . . I don't know, I felt really cheated.

RUTH: But that's life, isn't it? What relationship is ever truly resolved? People, perfectly likable people, inexplicably, inconveniently, behave badly, or take a wrong turn, or get sick and die. It happens. Besides, the final struggle in the story is an internal one—Martha's—and it's not *about* her illness, it's about her *inability* to tell her darling girl that she's very very sick. Those are two different things.

LISA: True.

RUTH *(Continuous)*: She can't bring herself to do it. She continually decides she's going to, in that last section, but she always loses heart. It's as if saying it out loud would make it too real. It would let death into the room, and she can't *do* that.

LISA: No, you're right. I see it now. You're absolutely right. In the end, what makes it so moving, is that you sense that this might be the very last cake the two women will get to bake together. That this prosaic little ritual is about to be wrenched apart. And it's very very sad.

RUTH: So you *were* moved by it.

LISA: Oh, God, yes. I was just mad at you for killing her off.

(A beat.)

RUTH *(Nods, her mood has become more solemn)*: Well, good. I'm glad you liked it. Thank you. Thanks for reading it.

LISA: You're very welcome. It was my pleasure. It was a real treat to read Ruth Steiner's latest, before anybody else.

RUTH: What you have to say means a great deal to me, you know.

LISA: No, I *didn't* know that.

RUTH: No? *(Lisa shakes her head)*: How could you not know that? It works both ways, you know. Am I supposed to just give and give and expect nothing in return?

LISA: No, of course not.

RUTH *(Continuous)*: I can't just applaud you and pat you on your back and offer unconditional love and support. *I* could use a little reassuring, too. *(Ruth is suddenly tearful)*

LISA: Ruth. What is it?

RUTH *(Shakes her head dismissively, then)*: This is complicated for me, you know.

LISA: What is?

RUTH: What's happening for you. It's very complicated.

LISA: Ruth? Are you jealous?

RUTH: Don't condescend.

LISA: I'm not. I'm sorry. I didn't mean to . . .

RUTH *(Over ". . . mean to . . .")*: It's not about envy—well, maybe it *is* about envy. But it's not pro*fessi*onal jealousy, it's . . . You know what it is? I'm jealous that you have all of life ahead of you. I can't sit back and watch you do the dance that I danced long ago and not think about time. I can't. *(A beat)*

That's what it's about. Don't you see? Time.

(Pause. She turns to Lisa and looks like she is about to say something. Lisa leans forward in her chair. Pause. Ruth changes her mind.)

Cheers.

(She downs her drink. The meaning of Ruth's behavior begins to dawn on Lisa as the lights fade.)

· Scene 2 ·

October 1996. Nearly two years later. The auditorium of the 92nd Street Y. Sound of applause. Lisa, wearing a flattering dress, nervously stands at a lectern and speaks into a microphone to the assembly.

LISA: Hello. *(She clears her throat, sips water)*

Hi. Thank you so *much* for that. It's so nice to be here at the 92nd Street Y, and be a part of this long literary tradition. I'm really honored. Thank you. I never expected such a turnout. Wow. I'm Lisa Morrison, by the way—just in case you're in the wrong room. *(A beat)*

Um . . . *(Takes a deep breath)*

I'm a little nervous. Forgive me. I'm new at this. I've never spoken in front of so many people before. I guess as long as I speak clearly, and with conviction, this should go reasonably well. It's important that you're able to *hear* me. At least that's what I was taught, and I was taught by a master. *(She scans the audience looking for Ruth, but doesn't see her. She takes a sip of water, then a deep breath)*

What I'd like to do, for starters, I'd like to begin with an extract from my new novel—what am I talking about?, my *first* novel, my *only* novel—*Miriam's Book*, which is being published next month by Viking? *(Corrects herself)* By Viking. And then, if my voice holds up—*(Clears her throat for effect)*—I thought I'd read one or two stories from my debut collection from a couple of years ago, *Eating Between Meals*. *(There is scattered applause, which surprises and amuses her)*

· 62 ·

Gee. Well! I feel like Joni Mitchell in *con*cert all of a sudden. *(Imitating a fan)* "Do 'Circle Game'!" *(A beat)*

Anyway, rather than describing too much about the book, I thought I would just start at the beginning. How's that? *(A beat)*

Miriam's Book. (A beat)

The prologue is titled "Night Falls Fast," which is taken from a poem called "Not So Far As the Forest" by Edna St. Vincent Millay that appears in the beginning. Do you know that poem?, are you familiar with it? *(A beat)*

Shall I read it? Okay, why don't I. *(A beat. Deep breath)* "Not So Far As the Forest"

(A beat. She reads; once she overcomes her nervousness, she reads quite well.)

That chill is in the air
Which the wise know well, and even have learned
    to bear.
This joy, I know,
Will soon be under snow.

The sun sets in a cloud
And is not seen.
Beauty, that spoke aloud,
Addresses now only the remembering ear.
The heart begins here
To feed on what has been.

Night falls fast.
Today is in the past.

Blown from the dark hill hither to my door
Three flakes, then four
Arrive, then many more.

(Pause. She sips water, then reads, with growing confidence.)

From the window of my apartment in Washington Heights, I can see a sliver of Hudson between two gray-brown buildings and, beyond it, the high-rise towers of northern New Jersey. It is a still and sticky September night and my window is open to the sounds and smells of West 174th Street. Across the way, down below, a souped-up car stereo blares salsa through a busted woofer while an overweight middle-aged couple dances on the sidewalk, spectacularly, in their bare feet.

The constant cries of ambulances, like loons in the city night, mingle with the radiant blast of music and the particular, gleeful noises of children at evening play. Somewhere out there, on this Indian summer night, in a narrow anonymous galley kitchen, someone is cooking with garlic.

I found my mind drifting tonight while reading or, rather, attempting to read a poem by one of my first-year Columbia graduate students, a dreary, earnest girl, who tries drawing a parallel between the sexual abuse she suffered as a child and the situation in Bosnia. The poem is unwieldy, pretentious and self-indulgent, but tomorrow, in tutorial, over mondel bread and tea, I will tell her it is *ambitious*.

I had gotten to the bottom of the third page and realized that I had absorbed not one word for some time. It was then that the timeless scent of garlic shocked my smelling sense and swept me, instantly, nine miles south and four decades back, to a crumbling but quaint railroad flat on Mulberry Street in the year nineteen hundred and fifty-seven.

I was young, very young, twenty-two in '57, a young twenty-two, not only a virgin but an innocent, a poet manqué from faraway Missouri, a Jewess from a place called St. Louis. New York had beckoned, like a beautiful dark lover with smoky breath and bloodshot eyes; I swooned and flew into his vampire arms with abandon, and left the stultifying beige safety of my parents' house forever.

The echoing sounds of colicky babies, wronged wounded lovers and Caruso on a crackling 78 greeted me as I first made my way up dim uncertain stairs to the unlikely garden of my new freedom. Giordano's Restaurant was on the ground floor. Angelo, the chef, got his marinara started at six every morning by throwing crushed garlic into a huge sauce pot of scalding oil. I could hear the sizzling meeting of garlic and olive oil upstairs, and imagine magnificent bursts of fireworks and symphonic crescendoes greeting each fistful. The aroma traveled through the screen door at the back, up the rusted fire escape, into my open window and caressed me as I lay in my bed.

So, when I am struck by the smell of garlic, as I was tonight, mixed with the dusty nighttime city air, I think of the intoxicating perfume of my youth, of that first summer on Mulberry Street, of long walks at all hours, of mildewy book stores, smoky coffee houses, of poetry and promise.

And I think of Emmett Levy.

Emmett Levy. Poet, madman, raconteur. The notorious and the legendary Levy. Great thinker, good poet, drunkard extraordinaire.

At forty-four, he had lived too long but would not die soon enough. His death would be ungentle, attenuated over nine desperate years, and I, a girl half his age, would see him through seven of his final seasons in a variety of roles: lover, nurse, mother-confessor, muse. I would love him and despise him, worship him and wish him dead. *(A beat)*

This is the story of those seven seasons in heaven and hell, so many years ago, when I was a girl of twenty-two, and lost my heart to a beautiful dark angel, a poet, named Emmett Levy.

(Pause.)

And that's the prologue. Shall I go on?

· Scene 3 ·

Later that night. Ruth's apartment. Ruth, wearing a cardigan over pajamas, stands at the window. Lisa opens the door but the chain is on.

LISA: Damn. *(Calls)* Ruth? Ruth, are you all right? *(Waits)* Ruth?

RUTH: Yes?

LISA: Ruth. Thank God. Open the door; the chain is on.

RUTH: What?

LISA: The chain, the chain is on the door.

RUTH: Oh. So it is.

LISA: Are you all right?

RUTH: Yes. I think so. As good as can be expected.

LISA: Are you going to let me in?

RUTH: Oh, I suppose so . . . *(She undoes the chain)*

LISA: Thank you. *(She's carrying a grocery bag)* Your door is usually open; since when do you use the chain?

RUTH: Only when I'm expecting burglars.

LISA *(Gives her a look; a beat)*: What happened tonight?

RUTH: What happened?

LISA: I was worried about you.

RUTH: *Were* you. I didn't say I'd make it for sure, I said I would try.

LISA: I know, but still, I was hoping. I guess you weren't feeling up to it.

RUTH: You could say that.

LISA: That's what I thought. *(An uncomfortable beat)* I brought you something.

RUTH: Oh?

LISA: I wanted to bring you something, I didn't know what to bring.

RUTH: What is it?

(Lisa removes a container from the bag.)

LISA: Cottage cheese. You said you had a craving for cottage cheese.

RUTH *(Over ". . . cottage cheese.")*: What size curd?

LISA: What?

RUTH: The curd, the curd. What size curd did you get?

LISA *(Looks at the label)*: Large.

RUTH: I prefer small.

LISA: Oh, of course. I forgot.

RUTH: How could you forget?

LISA: I wasn't thinking. I'm sorry.

RUTH: The hell with it.

LISA: I'll return it.

RUTH: Nah . . . Don't bother.

(Silence. Lisa senses the chill in the air.)

LISA: What would you like me to do? Would you like me to go down and see if I . . . ?

RUTH *(Over ". . . if I . . . ?")*: No no.

LISA: The Korean market is still open.

RUTH: Never mind.

LISA: Are you sure?

RUTH: I'm sick to my stomach anyway. Can't keep a goddamn thing down. I must have a calcium deficiency; I dream of dairy products. Forget it. If I don't eat it, Monica will.

(Lisa goes to put it in the fridge, she returns.)

LISA: Monica?
RUTH: My visiting nurse.
LISA: I thought her name was Beverly.

(She is picking up around the room: journals, periodicals, mail.)

RUTH: Beverly?! That was ages ago!
LISA: Sorry. I lost track. What happened to Beverly?
RUTH: Irreconcilable differences. Now I've got Monica. Who doesn't do housework. A big, beautiful, mocha-colored woman from Saint Kitts. With a bubbly, melodic voice. She calls me Mommy. "Are you hungry, Mommy?" "Are you cold, Mommy?" I hated it in the beginning: How dare this stranger patronize me like that? Then I started to like it. I *liked* being called Mommy. No one's ever called me Mommy before. *(A beat)* I don't see you anymore.
LISA: I was here last week.
RUTH: Not last week, couldn't've been last week.
LISA *(Over ". . . last week.")*: So maybe it was ten days ago.
RUTH: I'm telling you it's been *weeks*; Monica's been coming for weeks.
LISA: Has it really been that long?
RUTH: Yes!
LISA: I'm sorry; I've been busy. The book.
RUTH: Yes. Of course. The book. *(Pause; regarding Lisa's tidying)* Leave it.
LISA: You have junk mail here from Christmas.
RUTH: You don't have to pick up after me, I can still pick up after myself.
LISA: I'm just straightening up.

RUTH: Whenever *you* straighten up, things disappear.

LISA *(Flips through a* New Yorker*)*: Did you read the Janet Malcolm piece in here?

RUTH: Life's too short for the *New Yorker*.

LISA: It's good; you should read it. *(She puts it beside Ruth's chair)*

RUTH: I don't have time to read. I have all the time in the world and no time at all. My life is a paradox. That's quite a lovely dress you have on.

LISA: Oh, thank you.

RUTH: Looks expensive.

LISA: It was.

RUTH: That's what you wore tonight?

LISA: Uh-huh. I wanted to look *serious*—but sexy. Too much?

RUTH: For the 92nd Street Y? Perhaps. How'd it go?

LISA: Actually, it went fine. It was fun.

RUTH: Good.

LISA: There were a couple of candy-wrapper-crinklers I wanted to kill, but aside from that . . .

RUTH: I used to love readings. I always found them exhilarating. I loved playing all the parts. And getting laughs. I loved the laughter. I'm just an old ham, you know that.

LISA: Yes, I do.

RUTH: And it isn't just any old laughter; it's the self-congrat-ulatory laughter of people who want you to know that they get *every*thing.

LISA *(Smiles; then)*: This Barnard undergrad cornered me afterwards, saying she couldn't *wait* to meet me? It was really weird finding myself in a position of being pursued, when all my life I've been the pursuer—but she really wasn't interested in what I had to say; all she wanted was to talk about herself! *(Lisa observes Ruth lost in thought, not really listening. Pause)* Ruth? Would you like some tea?

RUTH: Hm? Thank you, I would. *(Lisa goes to the kitchen to put water on, etc. Pause)* You know? *(A beat)*

I . . . I should have had children of my own. It's my own damn fault. Too picky. I never met a man I could see myself having a child with. *(A beat)*

Nowadays the choice of partner would be totally irrelevant, I know, but it was a more conservative time then; things were different when I was ovulating. I should have just gone ahead and gotten pregnant with the next unsuspecting man that came into my life, snared him for his sperm and raised that child on my own. But I was never really the sort of woman who could do something like that. That would have required a brand of courage I sorely lacked. I was never truly Bohemian, never, that was all an act. A reaction to the fear, no doubt, of being hopelessly conventional.

(Lisa returns holding a saucer and a cup of tea.)

It would have been good for me, I think, having a child.

LISA: Yes?

RUTH: I might have become a different person. A better writer, maybe; a better human being, possibly. My life surely would have been *different*. Instead, I spent many many years, too many years, nurturing other people's gifted children. *(A beat)*

The first day of every class I ever taught—thirty-two years, thirty-two first days—I'd scan the faces and try to predict who out there would one day dazzle me. Who would thrill and astonish me with their promise? Who will it be this year? I'd want them, like a vampire wants fresh blood. I'd want to fill them up with what I know, these beautiful hungry empty vessels, and watch them grow. I've had a succession of chosen daughters through the years, mostly daughters. A few sons. Unformed, talented, as susceptible to my wisdom as I was to their youth. But none I loved as much as you.

LISA: Ruth.

(Pause.)

RUTH: I read your book.

LISA: Yes. I figured.

RUTH: Well, most of it, anyway. As much as I could possibly read right now. My eyes are stinging. There are tons of typos in the copy you gave me, tons.

LISA *(Over "... tons.")*: I know, it's an advance copy.

RUTH: I hope they're planning on correcting them.

LISA: Of course they are.

RUTH: I marked the margins anyway. Force of habit. There are some truly egregious errors in there.

LISA: I know.

RUTH: One whole section is suddenly repeated. I thought I was losing whatever mind I have left. Either that or you'd gone Joycean on me. And experimental fiction, as we both know, is not your style. *(Silence)* Lisa Lisa. If you had only asked me what I thought. If you had only asked me.

LISA: Ruth.

RUTH: I would have told you you were making a mistake.

LISA: I didn't know what to do, I didn't know how to handle it.

RUTH: Stay away from Schwartz; leave him out of it. He's mine, not yours. Besides, he's been done to death, picked over by so many vultures in the name of literature, and Bellow finished him off for everyone. If you had *asked* me. If you had only *asked* me.

LISA: Ruth.

RUTH: If you had only asked my advice. Forget my permission. If you had asked my advice. I'd have told you to look elsewhere, leave him alone, leave him out of it. They'll compare you to Bellow and your work simply can't support it, darling. It can't. You're not good enough. You may never be good enough. Why call attention to it? If you had asked me what I thought, I would have told you. But you didn't ask. Instead you skulked like a thief. Avoided me for two and a half years—

LISA: No, I didn't . . .

RUTH *(Continuous)*: —evaded my questions, failed to look me in the eye.

LISA: Ruth . . .

RUTH: You did, you did, my darling, I knew something was up: When you *did* come to see me, you couldn't *look* at me. I thought it was my appearance, that I was looking so awful you couldn't look me in the eye.

LISA: No!

RUTH: I could have used your friendship but you were too busy going through my panty drawer, scavenging through my personal effects.

LISA: That's not what I did!

RUTH: Then why did you skulk? Why couldn't you look at me?

LISA: I don't know, I . . . I needed some distance.

RUTH: "Distance"!

LISA: I needed to separate from you.

RUTH *(Amused)*: That you did, my darling, that you did.

LISA *(Over ". . . that you did.")*: You wouldn't know what it's like, to have to get out from under you, from under your influence, you couldn't possibly know what that's like!

RUTH *(Over ". . . what that's like!")*: Everything I told you. Everything I shared.

LISA: Ruth.

RUTH: What a fool I was.

LISA: No.

RUTH: It was all *material* to you! That's all it was.

LISA: That's not true.

RUTH: Here I was: regaling you with stories from my life like the pitiful old woman you've made me out to be . . .

LISA *(Over ". . . you've made me out to be . . .")*: "Pitiful"?! No, no . . .

RUTH *(Continuous)*: . . . and all the while you were taking notes!

LISA: That isn't true! I was listening! I was cherishing every minute!

RUTH: I'm sure.

LISA: If I had told you and you'd disapproved— *(Ruth turns away, busies herself)* Listen to me: If you had disapproved, I don't know what I would've done.

RUTH: Uh-huh.

LISA: I never could've written it. How could I have written it? I might have lost *you* and I would have lost my novel, too. I was scared.

RUTH: Poor thing.

LISA: I didn't know what to do! You were the one person who could advise me but I couldn't discuss it with you.

RUTH: Clearly you listened. You listened all right. You took it all in. And set it all out for the world to see.

LISA: What, what did I do that any good writer wouldn't have done?, that you wouldn't have done yourself? A story grabbed me and wouldn't let go.

RUTH *(Over . . . "wouldn't let go.")*: No, no, dear, that's where you're wrong: It didn't grab *you;* you *seized it,* it didn't seize *you.* Have you no conscience?! Have you no moral conscience?!

LISA: I have a conscience.

RUTH: *Do* you? *Do* you? You went ahead and did it anyway! That's what's so remarkable. You did it anyway.

LISA: What did you teach me: You taught me to be ruthless.

RUTH *(Struck by the unintentional pun)*: So to speak.

LISA: If something captures your eye, you told me, grab it. Remember? Like a good photojournalist: Go in and shoot. *(Ruth is evading her, Lisa follows her around the room)* Remember, Ruth?—Don't walk away!—That's what you taught me! Don't worry about feelings, you taught me that, worrying about feelings is sentimental and God knows we mustn't be sentimental.

RUTH: You've crossed the line, though, sweetie. You've crossed the line.

LISA: Why, because it involves you?

RUTH: I would think that would enter into it, yes! I was a fellow *writer* telling you these stories, not a longshoreman or a, a . . . *waitress*, for God's sake! A fellow writer! It's a matter of professional courtesy, I would think. What did I need to do?, proclaim them off-limits? Plant a flag? Make you *sign* something? You were my friend, goddammit!

LISA: I wish you wouldn't use the past tense.

RUTH: Once upon a time writers made things up, you know. Can you imagine?

LISA *(Over "Can you imagine?")*: Oh, come on. You used people all the time! Don't give me that shit. Whatever you could get your hands on, you took.

RUTH *(Over ". . . you took.")*: If I used people for my stories, my dear, they were people who *had* no voice, no outlet for expression.

LISA *(Over ". . . for expression.")*: Oh! Well! Is that so! That's awfully condescending of you, Ruth, really. How do you know? How do you know that?

RUTH: It's the truth!

LISA *(Continuous)*: You're always making these pronounce-
ments! When did the Little People you built your *career*
on choose *you* as their advocate?!

RUTH: I gave them a voice where they had none.

LISA: Well, there you go: We all play God. Don't we? We all
put words into peoples' mouths. You taught me that,
Ruth.

RUTH *(Over "You taught me that, Ruth.")*: No no no, what
you've done is something else, it's something else. I *have*
a voice. I *have* the tools.

LISA: Ruth . . .

RUTH: Use your own goddamn life! If yours isn't rich
enough, too bad; that's not my problem. Don't thumb a
ride and hop aboard mine. Hitchhiker!

LISA: Ruth! What do you make me out to be? You make me
sound like the most mercenary person imaginable. The
last thing I wanted was to hurt you.

RUTH: *Was* it? Oh, I don't know, I think you might be deceiv-
ing yourself, dear.

LISA: How?

RUTH *(Continuous)*: I think there's something terribly Freud-
ian going on here, don't you? The Oedipal struggle to
the finish. You destroy me and claim my lover for yourself, take him to bed with you. I think you *want*ed to
destroy me.

LISA: That's ridiculous.

RUTH: You wanted to obliterate me.

LISA: No, no, I wanted to *honor* you!

RUTH: *Honor* me?!

LISA: It was my gift to you.

RUTH: Your *gift*?!

LISA: Yes! I was honoring you. For all you've given *me*.

RUTH: Well, I don't want your gift. How do you like that?
I'm very sorry, that isn't very gracious, I know, but your

gift doesn't honor me. I want the receipt so I can exchange it for something else but you're telling me there *is* no receipt. It's take it or leave it!

LISA *(Genuinely)*: What exactly is so offensive to you? I don't understand it.

RUTH: You don't?!

LISA: No.

RUTH: You've stolen my *stories*, Lisa. My stories! What am I without my stories? I'm nothing. I'm a cipher. I'm as good as dead.

LISA: But they *aren't* your stories, Ruth. Not anymore. They stopped being your stories when you told them to *me*. They changed my life so how can they be solely your stories anymore? You don't *own* them.

RUTH: Oh, no?

LISA: No! You are a part of my life now, Ruth. Our lives intersect. My experience includes your experience. I am the sum of your experience and my experience and everybody else's experience I've ever come in contact with.

RUTH *(Over "... come in contact with.")*: Yeah yeah yeah.

LISA: I couldn't tell your stories, not the way *you* would, I couldn't *possibly* do that. But I *can* take your experiences, what I *know* of them, what I *make* of them, and extrapolate, *that* I can do, but my book doesn't pretend to be the *truth*. Miriam isn't *you*. *(Ruth scoffs)* She *isn't*.

RUTH: I know that line, *bubeleh*; believe me, I've used it.

LISA: All right, she's as much me as she is you.

RUTH: That lonely, pitiful woman, pining for Delmore Schwartz?

LISA: No, no, the young, impressionable disciple who wants nothing more than the high regard of her mentor.

RUTH: Is *that* what you were going for?

LISA: Yes!

RUTH: Then you've failed miserably; I don't see that at all.

LISA: That's 'cause you don't *want* to see it! You've totally, willfully, misread her! Miriam isn't pitiful. She's vital, funny, self-ironical. She sees the affair for what it truly was, in ways you obviously cannot!

RUTH: What is that supposed to mean?!

LISA: *You're* the one who calls it the "shining moment" of your life, for Christ's sake, Ruth!, that's what you told me! You wear it like some kind of masochistic badge of honor.

RUTH: Who the hell asked *you?*

LISA *(Over ". . . asked you?")*: You've let that one brief affair define your entire life!

RUTH: I have not! That is absurd!

LISA *(Continuous)*: You're like a professional war widow or, or Miss Havisham in her wedding dress or something!

RUTH: That is not who I am! That's insulting!

LISA: I'm sorry.

RUTH: You gonna lay some postfeminist crap on me now? Huh, Lisa?

LISA *(Wearily)*: No.

RUTH *(Continuous)*: How only *you*, with the benefit of a modern, feminist perspective, can put *my* affairs in their proper place? Is that it?

LISA *(Over "Is that it?")*: I wanted to reclaim for you a part of your life, okay? I wanted to give something precious back to you.

RUTH: Really! And who the hell asked you?! Who *asked* for your revisionism of *my* life?

LISA: Oh, boy . . .

RUTH *(Continuous)*: Not I. Not I. I've got news for you, kiddo, you wouldn't *be* where you so smugly sit if it weren't for women like me.

LISA: Yes, Ruth.

RUTH *(Continuous)*: It's our own damn fault: Our dirty work made your arrogance possible.

LISA *(Over "... possible.")*: Oh, please. Spare me the you-girls-have-it-so-easy shit.

RUTH *(Over "... -so-easy shit.")*: The way you take and take with this astonishing sense of entitlement! And not only have you usurped my love affair, oh no, but you've taken my entire *milieu* and passed it off as your own!

LISA: How? I don't know what you mean.

RUTH: You don't? Jewish intellectual life? New York in the fifties? Delmore is one thing, but to take on territory that is so identifiably mine?!

LISA: How is it yours? Do you have dibs on the entire spectrum of Jewish experience, too, Ruth? Exclusive rights?

RUTH: Look at my body of work! Look at it! You know it backwards and forwards, for Christ's sake!

LISA: You were a point of departure, like any inspiration.

RUTH: It's my *voice*, dammit! What you've done is mimicry, it's not art, it's not homage. It's parody. You had no right!

LISA: No right?! What about my right as an artist?!

RUTH: You have to *earn* that right! Who gave *you* the right to write about Jews?

LISA: What, because I haven't lived it I can't write it? Is that what you're saying? I can't write about Jews because I'm not Jewish? Do you really mean that?

RUTH *(Over "Do you really mean that?")*: I'm saying it's bogus coming from you. Inauthentic. Irresponsible.

LISA: And when *you* got into the heads of welfare mothers that was, what, social realism? Ruth, come on, you're not being fair. You're contradicting everything you ever taught me about writing!

RUTH: And what do *you* know about "fair"? The things you've got me doing, saying, thinking ...

LISA: Not you—*Miriam.*

RUTH: Either you're being disingenuous or very naive. Of course it's me. There is no fact, there is no fiction. The line is blurred. As far as everybody is concerned, it *is* me, so it might as well *be* me.

LISA: Ruth . . .

RUTH: Everybody knows you were my protégée.

LISA: So?

RUTH: So, you're pandering to the public. Like some tell-all rag.

LISA: No . . .

RUTH: *You* know how that is: You read a book and all the time you're guessing. You're smacking your lips and you're guessing.

LISA: So what? So what if they do?

RUTH: This is *my life*, dammit! You've appropriated *my life*! Maybe you thought it was up for grabs.

LISA: Ruth . . .

RUTH: Maybe you thought I was fair game.

LISA: No . . .

RUTH: Maybe you thought I'd be dead by now!

(A beat.)

LISA: That's a horrible thing to say! How can you say that to me?!

RUTH *(Over ". . . say that to me?!")*: Don't act so shocked, my darling, I'm sure it occurred to you, it would have occurred to *me* . . . *(A beat)* You've taken my life and turned it into pulp!

LISA: How can you call it pulp?!

RUTH: Forgive me, dear, but that's really what it is. Gossip. More grist for the mill.

LISA: Can't you tell it was written with love?

RUTH: Those sex scenes, Lisa! Oh dear God. Didn't I teach you *any*thing? What did I tell you about sex scenes? They always read like automotive mechanics, darling:

bodies and parts. *(Flipping through the book, paraphrasing)* That scene in the stairwell of her walk-up! *(Gasps)* The huffing and puffing! The creaking of the stairs! *Uy gevalt!*

LISA *(Making motions toward leaving)*: Forget it.

RUTH *(Continuous)*: His wet wool coat smothering her! His bear-like *huge*ness pressing pressing into her! Deeper and deeper and deeper! *(Ruth is laughing, almost maniacally, Lisa can't stand this but cannot bring herself to walk out. Pause)* He was impotent, darling. The great love of my life, your romantic hero. He was so destroyed by drink and Dexedrine by then, there *was* no sex, not sex as you so grotesquely imagined it, anyway.

LISA: So what? My book is fiction.

RUTH: Your "book" is shit. *(She tosses the copy to the floor. Pause. Lisa goes to it and picks it up. Silence)* You know what I would do if I were you, darling? Not that you asked me. If I were you, I'd buy back all the copies, every single one, and set a nice big bonfire in Tompkins Square Park. It shouldn't be a total loss: At least the homeless could warm their hands on it.

LISA: If I were in your place, if *my* life inspired a disciple of *mine* to write about it, I would be gratified.

RUTH: *Would* you?

LISA *(Continuous)*: I would be honored. I wouldn't be doing this.

RUTH: But the book isn't any good, Lisa. It's not gonna do you any good at all.

LISA: A lot of people would disagree.

RUTH: Pulp it. Shred it.

LISA: You know I can't do that; that's not an option.

RUTH: Work out a deal with your publisher. They're gonna take a bath on it anyway. Give back your advance. I'm sure they'd be delighted. They'll be getting off easy.

LISA: I can't believe you're doing this to me. You know how vulnerable I am . . . my first novel being published . . .

RUTH: I'm only telling you what I think would be the mature and honorable thing to do. Admit your failure, take the loss and chalk it up to experience. Admit your moral and artistic failure. Because if you don't, I'll do everything I can to stop it.

LISA: Stop it? What do you mean, stop it?

RUTH: *Stop* it! *Stop* it! I've spoken to my lawyer.

LISA: You what?

RUTH: Doesn't that sound corny? But I have; I called him today.

LISA: Oh, Ruth, this is foolishness.

RUTH: Is it?

LISA: I've done nothing wrong, nothing illegal. You have no legal grounds.

RUTH: I don't know, but I do have moral grounds. I still have sense and I still have friends and I'm gonna make a really big stink.

LISA: You don't want to do that . . .

RUTH: Oh, I do, I've got to. You've given me no choice.

LISA: You'll only get the opposite result. People will want to read the book. And *then* what would you have accomplished?

RUTH: I'm not gonna let you get away with this. People have got to know I was robbed.

LISA: You don't need that kind of publicity, Ruth. It'll be humiliating. A great teacher suppressing her student? The champion of free speech? It reeks of professional jealousy. You don't want to be remembered as a crank. I'd hate to think of you degrading yourself like that.

RUTH: And what have *you* done to me? Hm? What have *you* done?

LISA: You *wanted* me to write about him, didn't you.

RUTH: I what?!

LISA: "Don't talk about it, write it." Remember that, Ruth? That was one of the first lessons you ever taught me.

RUTH *(Over ". . . ever taught me.")*: Oh, please, you're gonna throw *that* in my face?

LISA *(Continuous)*: *Telling* a story takes away the need to *write* it, it relieves the pressure.

RUTH: You actually believe that shit?

LISA: Yes. Of course I believe that, Ruth. You taught it to me. *(A beat)* The day you told me about him I knew, by the *way* you told me, by the *language* you used. It had been written in your head long ago. When you said it out loud that day, when you released it, I knew, I could sense, that you were giving it to me.

RUTH: *Giving* it to you?!

LISA *(Continuous)*: You *wanted* me to use it.

RUTH: Bullshit! That has got to be the worst argument for theft I've ever heard! What are you saying, I left the window open?

LISA: I'm not saying it was conscious . . .

RUTH: Look, I'm perfectly capable of writing my own stories, thank you.

LISA: But, face it, Ruth, you were never gonna write this one.

RUTH: What?! Excuse me? How do you know that?!

LISA *(Over "How do you know that?!")*: I'm sorry, but it's true.

RUTH: What, do you think you know *every*thing about me? Do you think I was stupid enough to reveal *every*thing to you? How do you know I haven't already written it?

LISA: Ruth . . .

RUTH: How do you know I *haven't*? Maybe it's *here* . . . *(She pulls open a file drawer and tosses files to the floor)* Maybe it's right *here* . . .

LISA: Ruth, please . . .

RUTH *(Continuous)*: Maybe I *have* written it. Just because I didn't run to a publisher with it!. . .

LISA: Don't do this. *(Lisa touches Ruth's arm to calm her but Ruth violently pulls away. Silence)* This isn't about you and me, Ruth, and you know it.

RUTH: Oh, no? What's it about?

(A beat.)

LISA: It's about death.

RUTH: Death. Is it? I see.

LISA: Death is the third party here. You're angry at death.

RUTH: I'm angry at death. Thank you very much.

LISA: And I don't blame you, Ruth.

RUTH: You don't. How kind.

LISA: Please don't be angry with me. The last thing I wanted was for you to be angry at me. *(Pause)* I know the past few years have been a terribly rough time for you. I know that. And it pains me. It does. I'm so sorry you haven't been feeling well.

RUTH: I feel fine.

(Pause.)

LISA: What I mean is, I think it's the disease talking, Ruth, it's not you.

RUTH: I see.

LISA: It's clouded your thinking. You've displaced your anger onto me. And if that's what you need to do, fine, I'll take the beating. But I'm not your enemy, Ruth. I love you.

RUTH: You love me.

LISA: Yes.

(Pause.)

RUTH: Tell me: What did you think my reaction would be? Silence? Approval? What?

LISA: I don't know, I thought you'd feel . . . Pride. Satisfaction.

RUTH *(Incredulous)*: Satisfaction?

LISA: For having been a good teacher. *(Long pause. Lisa moves close to Ruth, puts her arm around her and holds her for a moment; Ruth doesn't respond)* Ruth. *(Silence)*

RUTH *(Exhausted)*: Go home.

LISA: What?

RUTH *(Breaking Lisa's embrace)*: I can't talk to you anymore.

LISA: Don't say that.

RUTH: Our trust is broken. I feel like I've been bugged. My dear young friend turned out to be a spy. A spy who sold my secrets.

LISA: Ruth, please. We can talk about this.

RUTH: Look, do me a favor, take out the trash with you, I've got a leaky bag.

(Silence. Lisa goes to the kitchen, returns with the trash bag and looks at Ruth for a long beat; Ruth's back is to her. Silence.)

LISA: Ruth . . . ?

RUTH *(Still facing away)*: Go home.

(Lisa takes her in for one last moment before leaving, then shuts the door behind her. Ruth is alone. Silence. The phone begins to ring; it rings many times. We think she may finally answer it but she doesn't. Lights fade slowly.)

END OF PLAY

DONALD MARGULIES was born in Brooklyn, New York, in 1954. He has received playwriting fellowships from the New York Foundation for the Arts, the National Endowment for the Arts and the John Simon Guggenheim Memorial Foundation. Mr. Margulies's plays have premiered at Manhattan Theatre Club, the New York Shakespeare Festival, South Coast Repertory, Actors Theatre of Louisville, Williamstown Theatre Festival and the Jewish Repertory Theatre. *Sight Unseen*, a Pulitzer Prize finalist, won The Dramatists Guild/Hull-Warriner Award and the OBIE Award for Best New American Play. *Collected Stories*, also a Pulitzer finalist, was named the Outstanding New Play of 1996 by the Los Angeles Drama Critics' Circle. A collection of his work, *Sight Unseen and Other Plays*, which includes *Found a Peanut*, *The Loman Family Picnic*, *The Model Apartment* and *What's Wrong with This Picture?*, is published by Theatre Communications Group. An alumnus of New Dramatists, he is a member of the council of The Dramatists Guild, and sits on the board of directors of Dramatists Play Service, Inc. He lives with his wife, Lynn Street, a physician, and their son, Miles, in New Haven, Connecticut, where he teaches playwriting at the Yale School of Drama.